Love in a Lunchbox

Poems and Parables for Children's Worship

Elaine M. Ward

ABINGDON PRESS
Nashville

LOVE IN A LUNCHBOX: POEMS AND PARABLES FOR CHILDREN'S WORSHIP

Copyright © 1996 by Abingdon Press

This book is printed on recycled, acid-free paper.

ISBN 0-687-00660-0

Cataloging-in-Publication Data is available from the Library of Congress.

Scripture quotations, unless otherwise indicated, are from the New Revised Standard Version Bible, copyright © 1989, by the Division of Christian Education of the National Council of the Churches of Christ in the United States of America.

Scripture quotations noted RSV are from the Revised Standard Version of the Bible, copyright 1946, 1952, 1971 by the Division of Christian Education of the National Council of Churches of Christ in the USA. Used by permission.

Scripture quotations noted GNB are from the Good News Bible—Old Testament: Copyright © American Bible Society 1976; New Testament: Copyright © American Bible Society 1966, 1971, 1976. Used by permission.

96 97 98 99 00 01 02 03 04 05—10 9 8 7 6 5 4 3 2 1

MANUFACTURED IN THE UNITED STATES OF AMERICA

For Lauren and Tiuh Ward,
B. C. Carlisle, Sara Aquilar, and
"grand children" who love stories
everywhere

Contents

Encountering God

Celebrating Lent: The Season of the Sacred Story

Engaging in Love

Participating in Prayer

Experiencing Wonder

Introduction

"The kingdom of God is like a story, which, when sown upon the soul, is the smallest of all the stories on earth; yet when it is warmed by wonder, watered with imagination, grows up and becomes the meaning of Existence, and puts forth a World of Possibility so that the creatures of the earth can make their homes in it." (paraphrase, Mark 4:30-32)

Children worship through their feelings. They sense the presence of God in the wonder of the world, in relationships of love, in participating in the words of the Bible sung and said and enacted, and in stories that offer them God's promise and plan in Jesus' birth, life, death, and new life.

Poetry is a region of the spirit. *Love in a Lunchbox* can help children enter the biblical story, engage in prayer and celebration of Advent and Lent, enjoy the stories and feel understood, and learn from example. Poems and parables may become models of meaning that form and feed children's faith as they pour light and possibilities upon our paths.

A defense trial lawyer told his pastor: "I took my defendant's case for the sole purpose of saving his life. But as the prosecutor stood before the jury I knew I had no defense. I could think of nothing to say to refute the arguments the prosecutor was proposing. 'Ladies and gentlemen of the jury, this man on trial took the wrong road from the beginning—the road of drugs, the road of robbery, the road of . . . '

"As he proceeded to enumerate the many and various wrong roads the accused had taken, I found myself, pencil in hand, making violent lines across the paper each time I heard the word *road*.

"Suddenly I stopped. 'What am I doing?' I asked myself. Instead of creating my line of defense, I was making marks on a piece of blank paper.

"I looked down at the paper. The lines, having been made from the word *road*, actually looked like a road. Into my mind flashed the story of another who had taken the wrong road. When I arose to address the jury, I knew what I would say.

" 'Ladies and gentlemen of the jury,' I began, 'there was once a man named Paul who took the wrong road, persecuting and killing Christians. His life was saved on the road to Damascus and he turned around. Who knows what this man before you might do if his life were saved.'

"I sat down."

As he told the story to his pastor, he added, "If anyone ever tells you Sunday school is a waste of time, that there is no value in hearing stories of the faith, just tell them that because of hearing the Bible stories as a child in Sunday school, a life was saved."

Love in a Lunchbox can be used for devotions, worship, and storytelling at Christian schools and day care centers, as well as in children's church, after school programs, vacation Bible school, day camps, children's time during the worship service, church school, and family gatherings. Each worship lesson suggests questions for the children to ponder without quick, ready adult answers, as well as discussion and participation.

Jesus told parables. Mark wrote that "he did not speak to them except in parables" (Mark 4:34). And John wrote, "These [stories] are written so that you may come to believe that Jesus is the Messiah, the Son of God, and that through believing you may have life in his name" (John 20:31).

TELL THE STORY

Taste a story,
Touch it,
Try it.
Tell the story,
Sell it,
Buy it.
Laugh a story,
Feel it,
Cry it,
Talk with it,
Walk with it—
And when you know your story well,
God fly with it!

Celebrating Advent:
Season of "The Story"

Advent Worship

Worship the LORD in holy splendor. (Ps. 29:2b)

It was Advent and we were worshiping. We were worshiping with our whole bodies, as well as with our minds and mouths. In the darkness we smelled the perfumed candles, the cinnamon and rosemary, and even the bitter herbs. We saw the red candles burning on the altar, the pink and white candles lighted on the Advent wreath, and the new banners announcing the birth of the Christ Child. We listened to the magnificent music of the prelude that helped us wait and long for Jesus' coming. We could almost taste our anticipation, when suddenly from the back of the church we heard bells ringing softly and approaching nearer, as the dancer in a long black dress gracefully moved down the center aisle, shaking her bells, smiling at each of us individually as she proceeded closer to the altar. The lights in the sanctuary went on one by one until she moved up the stairs into the chancel area before the altar, turning, and welcoming us to worship. Expanding her arms in a wide, welcoming gesture, her smile, her presence, and all of the lights filled the sanctuary with joy and peace, and we were in worship!

Questions to Ponder: Sit in silence with the story (or the enactment of it). Read the Bible verse slowly.

In worship we come into God's presence. Worship takes place at different times and in a variety of settings. In worship children sense the beauty and mystery of the world that cannot be explained in words. This sense of wonder and awe is the beginning of reverence for life and is the root of worship.

Movement in sacred dance or biblical pantomime appeals to the child's sense of sight.

Advent is the time of preparing for the coming of God in the birth of a baby. It is a time for establishing and renewing traditions, for children remember the emotions and the experience, the "feelings," long after they have forgotten the event.

The following are brief Advent worship services that invite your personal additions or substitutions.

(The Advent wreath has four red, or pink, or purple candles, one for each of the four Sundays before Christmas. The center candle is white and is lit on Christmas Day.)

Advent Worship Services

FIRST SUNDAY OF ADVENT

 Opening Words: "We have come together to think about Advent, getting ready for the birth of Jesus, God coming to live with us."

 Lighting First Candle: "We light this candle and thank you, God, for loving us."

 Sing: "Away in a Manger"

 Prayer: "Dear God, may our home (classroom) be filled with the love Jesus taught and lived. Amen."

SECOND SUNDAY OF ADVENT

 Opening Words: "This is the second Sunday of Advent." (Light first candle.)

 Lighting Second Candle: "We light this candle as we prepare for Christmas with love and joy."

 Sing: "O Little Town of Bethlehem"

 Prayer: "Dear God, we thank you for your love that is with us always. Thank you for Jesus who came to show us your love. Amen."

THIRD SUNDAY OF ADVENT

 Opening Words: "This is the third Sunday of Advent." (Light first two candles.)

 Lighting Third Candle: "We light this candle as we prepare to celebrate Christmas with love and joy and hope."

 Sing: "O Come, All Ye Faithful"

 Prayer: "Dear God, thank you for the love and joy of Christmas, the birthday of Jesus who taught us your love. Amen."

FOURTH SUNDAY OF ADVENT

 Opening Words: "This is the fourth Sunday of Advent." (Light first three candles.)

 Lighting Fourth Candle: "We light this candle as we celebrate Jesus' birthday."

 Sing: "Joy to the World"

 Prayer: "Dear God, thank you for Jesus and for this special day, Christmas. Teach us how to love. Amen."

CHRISTMAS DAY

 Opening Words: "This is Christmas Day." (Light the first four candles.)

 Lighting Center Candle: "We light this candle to say, 'Happy Birthday, Jesus.' "

 Sing: "Silent Night, Holy Night"

Prayer: Pray together the Lord's Prayer.

Advent is a time when the imagination comes alive, when the ordinary and extraordinary meet and become one, when stars sing and planets dance, and babies become kings and queens of earth, for Advent is the season of the heart.

Advent is also a time for "getting ready." For years the Hebrews waited and prepared for the Messiah. Children, impatient and eager creatures, know that same joy and frustration, and excitement and letdown. While we are getting ready for the arrival of unconditional love, let us enjoy the present as we wait and get ready for the future.

The day before Christmas, as well as the weeks during Advent, had been busy. Mother ran here and there, buying presents, baking, cleaning, wrapping presents, impatient of the interruptions of her daughter.

Father was busy, as well. The coming of Christmas only added to his duties, and so he had no time for the child.

It seemed to the child that she was in everyone's way, until she was hustled upstairs to bed. All the hurry and excitement of the day confused her and she knelt beside her bed to pray.

"God, forgive us our Christmases, as we forgive those who Christmas against us. Amen."

Baboushka

The fire crackled. The wind roared. There was a sudden knocking on the door.

"Who's there? Who's there?" cackled Baboushka from her rocking chair.

"We are shepherds from the hills come to tell the happy news."

"What is it? What is it, before I lose my patience?"

"On this happy, happy morn, in Bethlehem the king is born. Come with us to worship him in Bethlehem."

"I will. I will, but not until I sweep the floor, clean the cupboards, scrub the door. I will! I will!"

"Baboushka, Baboushka, the Baby cries for you."

"I will come . . . tomorrow . . . tomorrow will do!"

There was nothing more that they could say and so the shepherds went their way.

The sun shone. The flowers bloomed. There was a tapping at the door.

"Who's there? Who's there?" groaned Baboushka from her rocking chair.

"We are wise men from the east come to tell the happy news."

"What is it? What is it, before I lose my patience?"

"We have seen his star above and come to find the king to bring to him our gifts of love. Come with us, Baboushka dear, for the king is very near."

"I will. I will, but not until I bake a plumcake for the king and make the child a covering."

"Baboushka, Baboushka, the Child waits for you."

12

"I will come . . . tomorrow . . . tomorrow will do."

There was nothing more that they could say and so the wise men went their way.

When the house was spotless, the cupboards clean, and not a speck of dust was seen, when the cake was baked and the covering made, Baboushka packed her presents all, now to search for the stable and the stall.

But when she got there, the stable was bare and empty was the stall.

Through town and country, night and day, Baboushka wandered on her way, seeking, seeking, seeking.

So on each Christmas Eve, you may see sneaking up the stair a little wrinkled lady leaving her gifts there for every girl and boy to celebrate the joy of Jesus' birth, because Baboushka knows . . . tomorrow may be too late.

What are the gifts the lady brings?

Time to wonder, time to sing, hands to help, a loving heart . . . gifts suitable for a king.[1]

Questions to Ponder: What are the gifts the lady brings? Think of three gifts you would bring if you were Baboushka.

Spend time wondering, singing, and feeling "with a loving heart."

Christmas is a time for stories. The "good news," the message of God's love for us, came to us in a story of the birth of the Christ Child in Bethlehem. Stories picture eternal truths that can be taught and caught through the mind and the heart. A story can be a light to feed our spirit and enlighten our mind.

Advent is the season of hearing and telling the Nativity story. As Christians we are bound together by our sacred story. "Once upon a time" invites us to imagine and step into an uncharted place and time to enter the miraculous grace of the imagination and experience the desire and deliverance of a quest, a dream, or a longing. The joy of that deliverance will not last, but the memory, the sense of having had that joy, remains forever.

Stories that truly matter give "light" for our paths by revealing meaning. Where there is seeing and hearing with wonder a new aware-ness and dimension of meaning appears. What was not there before is there now. Yet it was there all along. Why did we not see it? Perhaps it is another example of "when the student is ready, the teacher appears."

Glory to God!

And suddenly there was with the angel a multitude of the heavenly host, praising God and saying, "Glory to God in the highest heaven, and on earth peace among those whom he favors!" (Luke 2:13-14)

This Sunday the angels would sing the sermon. The choir was singing a Christmas cantata for the glory of God. The pastor, with the children gathered around him at the altar, introduced them to the instruments that would be played, the choir, and the soloists who would sing, and then asked the children, "Why?"

They gave strange answers (only to be expected!), irrelevant answers, because the children did not know what answer the pastor wanted. I don't know if it was whispered from the choir loft (we were too far away to hear and the giggles drowned out the identity of the respondent), but someone said, "For the glory of God."

I wondered, and as Mary, I pondered the words in my heart, "What does 'glory of God' mean to a child?" So I told myself a story:

Once, in the darkness of time, in the fullness of space, God felt the tug of the smallest angel in heaven. With that tug of heart God knew the fullness of God's love for the world and for its creatures. Knowing their need for light, God sent the Light into that darkened world, and the heavens were filled with singing and the sky was split with song as the angels sang, "Glory to God!"

"Good news!" they cried, for Light had come to earth in the form of a baby.

The shepherds, watching their sheep that night, saw the glory of the Lord and heard the good news and ran to see this new thing that had come to pass.

They found Mary and Joseph and the baby lying in a manger, in a barn, because there was no room for them at the inn.

Questions to Ponder: The story is meant to inspire and to be pondered in silence. Invite the choir to sing a song of the Nativity in which the children can participate or appreciate in silence.

A story is a world into which children are invited. The child may not know the meaning of the word *glory* but the child sees with fresh eyes, hears with open ears, and feels the glory of our loving God and the Lord Jesus who is that story and that Light that enters the child's world. In that light we are transformed and become part of God's story, for that story of light and love says, "God is with us!"

Mary sang, "My soul magnifies the glory of God," and the angels sang with her, "Glory to God in the highest" (author's translation)!

> I thought I heard the heavens sing
> One lovely Christmas Eve.
> I looked about and wondered where
> The "heavenly hosts" could be.
> I stared into the sky, but there
> Was nothing I could see.
> I guess it must have been the wind,
> Or something . . . inside me?

God Was There

"Be still, and know that I am God!" (Ps. 46:10)

*I*t was the Sunday before Christmas. Amy was excited. The family had been too busy up until now to calmly appreciate the beauty of the season of Christmas with Amy. As Amy and her mother took their places in the dark, quiet sanctuary, neither spoke. They sat in the pew and **looked at** the Christmas wreath hung near the pulpit. They **smelled** the fresh pine needles of the large Christmas tree standing in the corner. They **enjoyed** the beauty of the burning candles on the altar. When the choir sang a Christmas carol, Amy moved closer to her mother. When the pastor told the story of Jesus' birthday, she **smiled**.

When they left, Amy put her hand into her mother's hand, whispering, "God was there."

Questions to Ponder: **Have you ever felt you were near or with God? Can you tell us about it?**
Repeat the story above, experiencing the boldface words.

In worship, children can experience the assurance of God's love and presence. Wonder is their worship. To tell children to be reverent is different from helping them feel reverent and in celebrating reverence with them. To help the child experience the biblical words, "Be still and know that I am God," or "Love one another" is a different approach from saying, "He's going to learn to love and share if I have to whale it into him."

Los Pastores

So they went with haste and found Mary and Joseph, and the child lying in the manger. (Luke 2:16)

*T*onight Los Pastores *begins. Perhaps this year they will knock on our door!" José said, wistfully. For as long as José could remember, he had wanted to hear the Christmas "knock" on his door. Tonight was December 16. Perhaps it would be tonight!*

Every year on December 16 The Shepherds, *an old Spanish play, was performed in José's neighborhood. For nine nights, from December 16 until Christmas Eve the story of Mary and Joseph on their journey from Nazareth to Bethlehem, searching for a place to stay in the crowded town, was acted out in Spanish-speaking communities.*

"Why do you think our poor home would be chosen as one of the Las Posadas (lodging)?" Dolores asked her younger brother.

"Our home may be poor but the Child loves the poor. He was born poor," their mother interrupted, secretly hoping with José that this year their door would be knocked upon by the strangers, seeking a place to stay. But José's mother knew that life holds both disappointment and joy.

Yet for weeks she had been making Christmas goodies just in case their home was chosen, for after the ceremony, the rest of the evening was spent playing games, dancing, and feasting together.

José quickly cleared the table and swept the floor. Pretending not to listen, he sat beside the door, studying his work for school the next day.

José could hear the sound of voices in the distance. Now the wheels of the small cart, containing the wax figures of Mary and Joseph, clattered down the brick street. The light from the candles of the men, women, and children who followed the cart filled the small room as the procession passed by.

"They didn't stop," said José sadly, as he closed his book.

"There will be other nights." Dolores was sorry for the way she had spoken earlier that evening.

"There are eight more evenings, José. Come, let us join the procession, too," his mother suggested.

The next night, while trying not to show his eagerness or his disappointment, José joined the celebration. José continued to join the celebration on the third night, and the fourth, and the fifth, and the sixth, all the while hoping that the next night would bring the knock on his door. But on the seventh night, when there was no knock on the door, and Dolores urged her brother, "Come, let us follow," José replied, "Not tonight."

Games and food for six nights had tired José and he went to bed early.

16

The eighth night José was so busy helping his mother with last minute Christmas preparations that he did not even glance up as the procession passed his door. Tomorrow was Christmas Eve and there was much to do.

"Buen Nacimiento," Dolores greeted her brother, the next evening.

"Buen Nacimiento," José smiled, bowing before his sister and kissing her hand as the Spanish gentlemen did.

"Buen Nacimiento," they called to their mother, planting a kiss on each of her cheeks.

Their gifts were few. Father had died when José was a baby, and Mother worked hard to feed and clothe them all. Their joys were in one another.

José heard the faint rumble of the cart in the distance. Mother heard it too and ran to the kitchen for food, in hopes of distracting José. Dolores began singing José's favorite Christmas carol. Without wanting to, José found that he was unable to resist singing and soon the house was full of the beautiful sounds of "Silent Night."

"José, stop!" whispered his mother. "I heard a knock."

"Listen!" Dolores warned. The singing stopped. They listened.

It was the most welcome sound in the world . . . a knock on the door!

As José opened the door, he remembered that he must refuse the holy family a place to stay. It was hard, after having waited so long. "There is no room!" he said.

José looked at the wax figures of Mary and Joseph in the cart. Again he repeated, "There is no room!"

José's heart beat faster. What if they should go away. "Come in!" he shouted. "Come in!"

"Buen Nacimiento," the people greeted one another.

The four men, carrying the cart, went to the empty manger and lowered the cart from their shoulders. José could see, for the first time, the figure of the Baby, as they gently lifted it from the cart, placing it in the empty manger.

It was the happiest moment of José's life, for the baby born in Bethlehem, God's gift of love, had come to José.

Questions to Ponder: Have you ever wanted and waited for something the way José did? Why did he want the baby at his house?

Los Pastores is a reenactment of Mary and Joseph's search for lodging on the night Jesus was born. Each evening from December 16 until Christmas Eve a procession of pilgrims seeks out a different home to ask for shelter.

The Franciscan friars, who brought Christianity to the New World, developed this tradition in their missions as a way to teach the people the story of the birth of Jesus.

The Baby in the Manger

"This will be a sign for you: you will find a child wrapped in bands of cloth and lying in a manger." (Luke 2:12)

The sanctuary was decorated with flaming red poinsettias and blazing lights. The children, parents, grandparents, and friends filled the sanctuary with the sound of the old familiar, favorite Christmas carols about the newborn baby in the manger. It was Jesus' birthday.

The kindergarten children acted out the Christmas story of the Baby's birth, as the minister read from the Bible the story of God's love for the world, and Mary smiled down at her baby in the manger.

Then it was over, the lights went out, the sanctuary was quiet and empty, except for the doll in the manger.

The children rode home with their parents, excited over their evening's celebration of the baby Jesus' birth, all but Elizabeth. Elizabeth had played the part of Mary in the pageant, and now she was crying softly as she rode home in the car.

"What's the matter, Elizabeth?" her mother asked.

"Who will take care of the baby? The baby is alone in the dark church," Elizabeth sobbed.

Into the dark, empty sanctuary Elizabeth and her family returned to care for the baby in the manger, and God smiled, for at least one child understood the meaning of God's gift of love.

Questions to Ponder: What is God's gift of love to you? How do we say "thank you" to God?

The baby in the manger reminds us that God loves, that God is involved in our competitive, complacent world, and that sometimes it is "angels in pinafores" that show us how to love.

Children enjoy stories by participating in them. The three year olds gathered around their teacher to hear the story of the angels singing the good news of Jesus' birth, of the shepherds running from the hillside in the dark night to the quiet stable, of the star that shone so brightly over the manger bed, and of the stall where the sheep and goats and cows surrounded the small baby, his mother Mary, and his father Joseph, that first Christmas morning in the little town of Bethlehem.

The children listened carefully. They listened with their ears. They listened with their eyes. They listened especially with their imaginations. They listened as long as young children could listen and then they moved.

Some went to build a stable with the blocks. Some scribbled pictures of bright stars. Some fingered the crèche figures and rocked the baby in their arms.

Lennox went to the housekeeping center and upon seeing the telephone, called out, "I am going to call Mary."

Mary must have answered immediately, for Lennox continued without a pause, "Mary, I just wanted to know how the baby is doing."

Courtney, watching Lennox, shouted from the other side of the room. "Let me talk to Mary. Is Jo-seph there, too?"

Out of their imaginations Lennox and Courtney and the other children began creating the biblical story of the first Christmas.

The Colors of Christmas

Tell the Nativity story with the Bible in your lap (Luke 2:1-20). Telling the story helps children understand that it is "your story."

Show colored pieces of cloth as you read the following poem the first time. Before reading the story a second time, distribute rhythm instruments, asking the children to help you tell the story by saying, "I will nod to you when it is your turn to play your instrument softly."

> Each color has a feeling,
> Each color has a smell,
> Each color has a story
> That they tell. (jingle bells)
> White the moonlight, white the dove, (triangle)
> While the angels sing above
> Pure and white,
> That Christmas night,
> Telling shepherds of God's love.
> Blue . . . the wing of a bird, (autoharp)
> The sea, the sky,
> Blue is the mother Mary's cry
> In reply to the cold and careless town,
> Blue is the color of her gown.

19

The red sunset (soft drum)
Reminded him of home.
How far they had come!
The sand too was drenched in red,
The rocks, the stones.
They talked in quiet tones,
Walking their way to Bethlehem.
The fire burning within his heart,
Joseph prayed, "God, let me do my part."
Brown, brown, the shepherds' coats, (sandblocks)
Brown their sheep and brown their goats,
Brown the stable, brown the hay,
Brown the manger where he lay.
Sand and dust and trees and ground,
God must like the color brown.
Gold is the color of the coin of a king, (cymbals)
Some people think gold can buy anything . . .
Fame and friendship, forgiveness, joy,
A faraway castle, a magic toy,
Love and wisdom, travel abroad,
Once wise men used it to praise their God!
Each color has a feeling,
Each color has a smell.
At Christmastime the colors have
A story that they tell. (play all of the instruments)[2]

Questions to Ponder: **Do you prefer to listen or to do? What do you like most about Christmas? What is your favorite color? Why?**

Children learn what they do. They learn through their senses and they remember when they participate. In participation children move. Life is movement. When God created, God moved. Movement is a part of religious expression. We are people with bodies. Moving is inseparable from children's exploring, experiencing, and experimenting.

The Enacted Story

In those days a decree went out. . . . (Read the entire account of the Nativity in Luke 2:1-20.)

It was a joyous, frightening Christmas Eve,
Ideally made for white-robed angels

Wearing silver tinsel in their hair,
And hooded shepherds, tennis-shoed,
Whose eyes showed eager expectation,
Holding woolly lambs within their care.
My camera caught the wise man's satin robe,
The light upon his shining vessel,
The glitter of his golden crown,
The smile upon his face,
The drummer boy in stockingcap,
Whose gift of sound flowed through the silent place.
And yet I could not capture there
The feelings that they held inside,
Or those they brought to grandmas, parents, friends,
No more than they who wrote the story
Of the night the angels sang and shepherds ran to see a king,
For no one comprehends the glory
Of the story that God sends.

Questions to Ponder: **Were you ever in a Christmas pageant or play? What do you remember? Who were you? What is the meaning of Christmas? What do you enjoy most about the Nativity story?**

If the children are leading worship by enacting the Nativity story, the poem might be read at the close of the service. Sometimes children are disappointed when they are not chosen to be Mary or Joseph. Is it possible to have in your enactment all the three- and four-year-olds as angels, five-year-olds as donkeys, the six-year-olds as Mary, and so on, according to the way the children are grouped in your church?

The most concrete thing we know about Jesus is that he was a storyteller. As Madeleine L'Engle once said, "Jesus was not a theologian. He was God who told stories."[3] He was the story that God sent.

Stories help us cast out demons and become aware of angels in our midst. They can heal us, lead us, implant hope in us, comfort, challenge, and correct us.

God speaks to us in stories that invite us to see what we might not otherwise see. They tease the imagination into transformation. The Advent story enacted by children helps us see God's glory.

Jesus' stories invited his hearer to become imaginatively involved. "Try seeing it this way. What do you see?" "Here is another image of possibility," or "This way to the kingdom," which is not a place, but the presence of God among us, within us, outside of us.

21

The Real King

I am king!" Alan shouted, holding the plum before them all.

It was the celebration of Epiphany, the "showing" of God in Jesus the Christ, the celebration of the three kings, when whoever found the plum in his or her cake became king or queen for the occasion.

"I am king," Alan said again, this time to himself. "A king has power. I am proud to be king. I am king," he announced to his people, but no one replied, and one by one they turned away. Alan was king without a kingdom.

"I will wage war and give my people something to do." He ordered everyone to come and be part of his army, but no one came.

"I will create laws. The people must obey the king!" Alan would decide who should do what and when and where.

But no one listened to the laws, so no one obeyed the laws. Therefore Alan decided to tax his people, but no one paid the taxes.

Remembering that his becoming king was part of the celebration of the wise men's finding the Christ Child, Alan found the wisest person he knew and told her what had happened. "I am king, but no one listens or obeys."

The wise woman smiled at Alan and said, "You failed because a real king creates peace, rather than war. A real king creates love rather than law, and a real king collects wisdom rather than wealth. Yet you can still rule."

"Tell me how. Will I be given a second chance?" Alan asked.

"Every girl and boy, woman and man is meant to rule wisely, to be king or queen of the kingdom that lies within each of us. Yes, you have another chance to rule your kingdom with peace and love and wisdom."

And so he did, and he became the Christ for his neighbor, who is, of course, the real king.

Questions to Ponder: How are we like "kings" and "queens"? Who is "the real king" for you, meaning someone you would follow? What gifts might you bring your king?

Sing "We Three Kings."

The season of Epiphany is celebrated in the Epiphany story of the wise men coming to find Jesus and to share their gifts of gold, frankincense, and myrrh. In some churches they celebrate the story by baking a plum in an Epiphany cake. The one receiving the piece containing the plum is "the king or queen" for the occasion.

The Three Magi: Epiphany

Based on Matthew 2:1-11.

Characters: A narrator, three wise men (or women) called the three Magi: Faith, Hope, and Love. Each wears a placard stating his or her name, as they walk down the center aisle, talking together.

Faith: We saw it! We did see it! Remember the night when the warm breeze blew in from the sea and the star seemed to say, "Have faith, come, follow me!" (Shake fist in faces of other two with great excitement.)

Hope: I hope so. We have traveled so far all I have left is hope.

Narrator: The days since the Magi left on their search for the Child by following the star had lengthened into months, and months into years.

Faith: I believe. I have faith that we will find the Child.

Hope: I hope so. I only hope so!

Faith: It is not hope but faith that matters.

Hope: I hope so. (Shake head.)

Faith and Hope: Yet we would not have reached this far, had it not been for your love and care. (Turn toward Love.)

Faith: Remember the night you traveled through dark and dangerous woods to get us medicine to heal our sickness?

Hope: And when we had no food, you begged among the people.

Faith: I have faith you will be rewarded.

Hope: I hope so, too!

Narrator: The third Magus smiled his (her) appreciation.

Faith: We will soon be there! I know we will!

Hope: I *hope* so! (Speak slowly.)

Love: But look, the star has disappeared.

Faith: No, I see a faint light ahead over the small village we are approaching.

23

Hope: I hope so (enthusiastically).

Narrator: As the Magi came into the village, they saw that the people there were very poor and dirty. The beggars crowded around the three Magi, begging for money and food.

Faith: I have faith the star will come again.

Hope: I . . . I hope so.

Love: Look, the people need us here. This is where we belong. Let us stay here and share what we have.

Narrator: The three Magi agreed. Faith lifted the children onto his (her) camel and told them about the special star and the importance of faith to make the impossible possible. Hope sat in the center of a group of the village elders and told them of the importance of the persistence of hope. Love fed and healed the people.

The three Magi were so busy showing faith and hope and love that they did not even notice that the star had reappeared, for they no longer needed it. Their search for the Child had ended. The Child was here among them in Faith and Hope and Love.

Questions to Ponder: **What is the "star" you follow? The wise men followed a star. A star could be a metaphor, a word to stand for Jesus Christ who said, "Follow me." How do we "follow" Jesus?**

The Star

On my tiptoes
I can reach
And touch the Christmas star.
Stretch a little
And you'll find
Your dream right where you are.

Questions to Ponder: **What is the meaning of Christmas for you? "To stretch" means to keep moving toward something you love.**

Poetry helps stretch children's minds and imaginations and Christmas is the time to hear and speak and write poetry, for Christmas is God the Poet sending the poetry of Christ into the world as history.

Poetry helps children become sensitive to the power and music of words. It equips us to live fully. A man at a spiritual growth retreat was reading a book of poetry, when another, seeing his book, said, "That book will never save your soul." The reader replied, "But it will make my soul worth saving."

Wishing

This is what we pray for. (2 Cor. 13:9b)

The bulletin board was covered with a rainbow of red, orange, yellow, blue, and green, and surrounded by yellow Christmas stars. The words over the rainbow read: "When You Wish Upon a Star," and on each star was written a child's wish.

Some of the stars said, "I wish I had a baby horse . . . a puppy . . . a baby sister . . . lots of candy . . . new shoes. . . . Kelly's read: a snail.

I admired the beauty of the board and as I read the stars, I enjoyed the children's wishes. That evening my son, sitting outside, saw a snail oozing across the sidewalk. He casually reached for the snail to remove it.

"Stop!" I cried. "Wait!" I ran to the kitchen for a container.

The next day I brought Kelly his wish.

I learned that day that wishes can only be fulfilled by others when you share them.

Questions to Ponder: Have you ever wished upon a star? What wish can you share? What do you think of or feel when you see a star? What did the star in the Christmas story in the Bible mean? What did it do?

Cut out paper stars and write on each a good thought or wish for each child. Place the stars in a container and invite each child to take one and ponder, wish, or pray for, on their star.

Or, substitute the following story:

The Star in the Apple

Once upon a while ago there was a little girl who had nothing to do. She asked her mother what she could do and her mother said, "Go out and find a little round, red house, with no doors, no windows, a chimney on top, and a star inside." The little girl went out and asked the first person she saw. "Have you seen a little round, red house, with no doors, no windows, a chimney on top, and a star inside?" Everyone she asked said, "No, but go ask . . ." (Use familiar names of people to ask. When you have run out of people to ask, end with, "Go ask Granny.")

So the little girl skipped to Granny's at the foot of the hill. "Granny, have you seen a little round, red house, with no doors, no windows, a chimney on top, and a star inside?"

"Yes," said Granny and she gave the little girl a round, red apple.

The little girl put the apple in her pocket and returned home. "Mother," she cried, "I found a little round, red house, with no doors, no windows, and a chimney on top, but how do I know if a star is inside?"

Her mother went to the kitchen and took a knife. She cut the apple open and there inside was . . . a star!

Questions to Ponder: **What did the little girl want? What did her mother tell her to do? (Cut an apple open and show the star within.) What does the star inside the apple remind you of?**

Some of the children may recall: "Star light, star bright, first star I see tonight. I wish I may, I wish I might, have the wish I wish tonight." Talk about the children's wishes.

Wishing is a normal activity for children. As adults we remember wishing on the first star, the wishbone of the chicken, or a magic penny. Christmas is a time for wishing, for dreams, as well as for giving. We are people with both a "need-love" and a "gift-love." Out of the experience of being loved we receive the ability to give gift-love. In the Bible verse above, Paul writes of "praying," which the King James Version of the Bible translated "wishing."

Wishing and imagination seem to go together. Hopelessness usually involves a constriction of the imagination. Wishing opens the imagination. A wish is a movement toward God and toward the world. The best and most human part of us is the ability to wish. From wishing on the first star to the chicken bone to petitionary prayer, we wish. Not to wish is not to have hope.

Entering the Bible Story

As we share biblical stories with children, we open a door into another world. Most children do not confuse reality and fantasy. They know that lions eat men, fire burns, and giants destroy. They also know, without having been told, that trust in God closes lions' mouths, puts out fire, kills giants. With time it is by such stories as "Once upon a time . . . there was a perfect garden, two brothers walked in a field, a snake spoke, some people decided to build a tower, there was a flood," and so on, that children hear and arrive at the gospel "truth."

Dr. Bruno Bettelheim in *The Uses of Enchantment* tells the story of the reaction of a five-year-old boy whose mother, encouraged by reading and discussion of the importance of stories for children, overcame her hesitancy about telling "threatening" stories to her son. She knew from speaking with her son that he already had fantasies about eating people or of people getting eaten. So she told him the story of "Jack the Giant Killer." At the end of the story the boy responded, "There aren't any such things as giants, are there?" Before the mother could reassure him, which would have destroyed the value of the story for her son, he continued, "But there are such things as grownups, and they're like giants."

Bettelheim wrote: "At the ripe old age of five, he understood the encouraging message of the story: although adults can be experienced as frightening giants, a little boy with cunning can get the better of them."[1] David with a slingshot and trust in God "got the better" of his giant.

Bible Stories

The boy who left his father's home,
The man who lost his sheep,

27

The stories in the Bible are
One way we hear God speak.
The person who was neighbor to
The man who needed care,
These stories Jesus told his friends
To help them love and share.
The day the happy children came
To him so eagerly,
But Jesus' friends turned them away,
'Til he said, "Come to me!"
The story of that Christmas Eve,
When shepherds ran to see
The baby Jesus in the hay,
Loved by his family.
There's Abraham and Samuel,
And Peter, John, and Paul,
And Joseph, Moses, David, Ruth,
I wish I knew them all.
For each of them were very close
To God, who's always near,
And speaks to us through people and
The Bible words we hear.

Questions to Ponder: **Place a Bible in a paper bag and give each child a turn to feel inside the bag and guess what it is. Ask them not to say what it is aloud until everyone has had a turn. After the last child has had a turn, ask them, "What did you feel in the paper bag? What is the Bible? What is your favorite Bible story?"**

Ask the children to pray with you: "Dear God, we thank you for this book of stories about your love and plan for us. We thank you for our parents and friends around the world and ask that you help us to love them. Especially we thank you for Jesus and his love for all people. Amen."

The early biblical stories are symbolical truths that can be expressed in no other way. They speak to the inner self. Facts are outside, truth is within. It is the "truth" of the Bible, "God is love," "God cares about you" that we share as we use the Bible with children. We ask, "Will this story (pictures in the mind) help children trust or will it cause them to question God's abundant love for all people?"

There are different levels of hearing a Bible story. We peel away its layers as the skins of an onion:

The *first level* is hearing the story as a story, a story with a plot and characters who act and feel and think.

The *second level* of a story is its meaning. What does the story mean to me? To the people to whom it was told? For whom it was written? Interest in meaning comes later, although it varies with individual differences. Around the fourth grade a sense of history about past events comes into children's awareness.

The *third level* is the value of the story. How am I related to this story? How is this story *my* story? What does it tell me about God in relationship to me and my experience? How do I live out the value and meaning of this story in my own life?

It would be unwise not to be aware that we leave out parts of the biblical stories or rather, save them, until they are of meaning and value to the person hearing them. Yet we continue to tell and hear the stories together, for young children too, are part of our communities of faith that grow up around the story, the story of God's "beginning" in creation, whose "plot" moves to its "climax" in Jesus Christ, and whose "ending" goes on and on and on.

The Lost Sheep

He [Jesus] told them this parable: "Which one of you, having a hundred sheep and losing one of them, does not leave the ninety-nine in the wilderness and go after the one that is lost until he finds it?" (Luke 15:3-4)

*C*harlie! Charlie!" *The shepherd called his sheep. Charlie liked to wander.*

Every day the shepherd brought his sheep to the hills to drink the cool water from the fresh stream and eat the crisp, green grass.

Every night the shepherd brought his sheep down the hill to the sheepfold to sleep.

The shepherd loved his sheep very much. Charlie, however, was different from the others and needed special attention. While the sheep nibbled grass on the hillside and drank water from the stream, Charlie would explore and discover new things.

"Charlie, come back!" the shepherd called again. After Charlie scampered back and began nibbling the grass with the others, the shepherd could sit back on the hillside and sing songs of praise and joy to God, his Good Shepherd.

"The Lord is my shepherd," he sang, "his rod and his staff comfort me." The shepherd looked at his staff, sometimes called a rod or a crook, and remembered how he used it to fight and frighten the wild beasts that would come upon the

29

sheep. Then suddenly he noticed it was getting dark. It was time to take the sheep to the sheepfold where they would be safe for the night. In the dark, wild animals could catch the sheep and eat them.

That night the shepherd counted his sheep, "ninety-seven . . . ninety-eight . . . ninety-nine . . . " The shepherd had taken one hundred sheep to pasture, but now one of them was missing. It was Charlie!

The shepherd was hungry and tired but Charlie needed him. He returned to the dark hills calling, "Charlie! Charlie!" For a long time he called and searched. He loved Charlie even though he caused him so much trouble.

For a sheep, Charlie had a lot of curiosity, but he had always been there when it was time to go down the hill.

"Charlie! Charlie!" the shepherd called again and again. He was a good shepherd to come back to the hills in the dark to look for his lost sheep. He was hungry and cold and tired, too.

When he heard the mountain lion roar, he called even louder.

"Where is Charlie?" he thought. "He must be afraid." "Charlie!"

"Baaaah." The shepherd ran to the sound.

Charlie was caught in a bramble bush. The shepherd took his staff and stretched it into the bush and gently pried him loose and then cuddled him in his arms. "Charlie!" he said, softly.

"Baah." The sheep felt safe and contented. It was good to be safe in the shepherd's arms. It was good to be under the loving care of a good shepherd. It was good not to be lost any longer.

Questions to Ponder: Have you ever been lost? How did you feel? What happened? How do you think Charlie felt being lost in the dark, hearing the roar of the mountain lion? How is God like a shepherd? By what name do you describe God? What does the word "God" mean? Who is God? We give many names to God, many words that try to describe who God is by what God does.

The biblical stories have survived the slings and stings of criticism, the psychological punchings and probings, and so on, for they have their origins, their heritage in the universal story, telling truths that can only be told and experienced in this way, stories that connect us with one another. The biblical stories connect the reader/hearer with mystery and God: a talking snake, a burning bush that was not consumed, a great sea parting so God's people could walk through and escape from bondage, a boy killing a giant and saving his people, another boy taken from a pit to become a king who saved not only his people but the Egyptians as well, lions' mouths being closed, men in fiery furnaces singing, animals riding in a boat, people outriding a flood, Jonah in a fish, the melodic sound of the psalms, and a baby Savior born in a stable, who grew up to struggle with Satan, walk on water, change water into wine, and to tell wonder-filled stories that led to his miserable death on a cross. And then a resurrection, and most wondrous of it all, behind and above and within . . . God. The Bible contains the core stories around which our communities of faith are formed and of which we are formed. We are called to tell the story.

While hiding from enemies in the hills and caves of Judah, David composed Psalm 63. He began: "O God, you are my God." David the singer, the psalmist, named the God he worshiped "my shepherd." When Moses asked God what he should say when the Israelites asked for God's name, God said to Moses, "I AM WHO I AM" (Exod. 3:14). And in the book of Isaiah, the King of Israel said, "I am the LORD, and there is no other" (45:18). Jesus called God the "Good Shepherd."

David and the Giant

"You come to me with sword and spear and javelin; but I come to you in the name of the LORD of hosts, the God of the armies of Israel." (1 Sam. 17:45)

D*avid, you should see him. He's as big as a mountain!"*

"Oh, come now."

"Well, he is as big as a bear and as loud as a lion and all our armies are afraid of him!"

David, being too young to fight in the army, carried food from home to his brothers, who were soldiers.

"Why doesn't someone fight Goliath?" David asked, for the giant's name was Goliath.

"Wait until you see him!" they told David.

David did not have to wait long. "Where is he who will fight Goliath?" The sound shook the hills. The men ran away with fear and trembling.

"How can one man frighten the armies of the living God?" David asked the men, when they finally fell to the ground in exhaustion.

"If you think you're so brave, go tell the king you will fight Goliath yourself!"

So David went to the king, who of course refused to let him fight. "You are but a boy, a small boy. Stick to caring for your sheep."

"When the lion takes a lamb from my flock, I go after him and fight to take the lamb from his mouth, with God's help. With God's help, I will fight Goliath."

31

King Saul said, "Then take armor and sword and go." He would not be mocked by a young boy.

But the armor and sword were too heavy for David so he chose five smooth stones instead and put them in his shepherd's bag.

"Am I a dog that you come to me with sticks?" roared Goliath.

"I come to you in the name of God," David replied, placing one of the stones in his sling. Before the giant knew what hit him, he was on the ground at David's feet.

Questions to Ponder: **What do you think Goliath looked like? Why did David want to fight Goliath? What would you have done? Why?**

Sharing the biblical stories that teach children to trust in God are often couched in symbolism and metaphor. We do not use them to give children packaged answers, but to invite them to go within themselves to listen to the sounds of their own hearts.

Because of its violence many adults have stopped telling the story of David and the Giant. It is, however, an encouraging story for children to hear. It is not the violence of the story that attracts them (they see an abundance of that on television and in real life), but that David outwitted the giant, the Big One. With a handful of pebbles, a sling, and faith in God, a child took on and accomplished a task too difficult, too formidable for the adults. A hero story is a vital necessity in difficult life conditions, for we need models in order to hope and to cope. A hero story is something to live for and be encouraged by. Such stories provide creative possibility. Research shows that rather than putting things into the child's mind, these stories objectify contents that are already there.

How does the *small* child fight the *huge* enemy? How does a minority group face their larger majority opposers? What does it mean to trust God when there is individual and cosmic danger? What is the symbolical message of the biblical story of David and his giant for you?

Such stories strengthen imagination and imagination encourages the development of the child's inner resources, the power to hope and cope. Children face internal and external fears and dangers. Through play, story, and the use of the imagination, they can work through these fears. "I'm a giant . . . a 'David' . . . a big dog . . . a doctor. . . . "

Fantasies are healthy for emotional growth, because it is unacceptable to act out violence. Such stories are symbolical, suggesting inner conflicts, life as it is seen or felt from the inside. Biblical stories answer some of the child's most important questions and needs.

Children love the story of David and the giant Goliath because one of the developmental tasks of children is to prove their strength. Thus, the child is emotionally involved with heroes of strength, such as the boy David.

Reading is not the same as being told the story, because while reading alone the child may think that only some stranger (the author of the book) approves of a young boy who outwits and cuts down the giant. But when his parents (teachers or pastor) tell him the story, the child can be sure that those close to him approve of his fantasy retaliation against the threat of adult dominance.

The hero or heroine is the restorer of health, incarnating healing, putting the hearer emotionally back on his or her feet. Through the story, children hear "You can do it too!" and in the church, children hear the greatest rescuing story of all, the story of God's love in the death and resurrection of Jesus the Christ.

Abraham

Now the LORD said to Abram, "Go from your country and your kindred and your father's house to the land that I will show you." (Gen. 12:1)

There once was a man who heard the word of the Lord. He was a happy man. He had a loving family, a good job, and many friends.

"Why me, Lord? There are so many others. Why me? Choose someone younger, Lord, someone who has more energy and strength. Choose someone older, Lord, someone who is wiser and more mature."

But he couldn't get away from the word of the Lord.

"Later, Lord, I will be glad to do what you ask. It's just not convenient now. I am responsible for Lot, and his children need to be cared for. My father is old and should not travel. Lord, I am needed in my work here."

But he couldn't get away from the word of the Lord.

He bought himself a new camel and rode around the city with great joy and pride, but he couldn't get away from the word of the Lord.

He held a great banquet and invited all of the important people in the town, for they were his friends. They ate and they drank and they had a merry time, but he couldn't get away from the word of the Lord.

He went to the temple and watched the people worship. He watched them worship their statues, their idols, and he laughed, for he couldn't get away from the word of the Lord.

The Lord had said, "Go! Leave this land of idols, of false gods, and worship me!"

The Lord had said, "Be the father of a new people, the father of my people!"

The Lord had said, "Build me an altar wherever you are, and I will be with you!"

Still the man couldn't get away from the word of the Lord.

So Abraham left his land and traveled across the long, hot desert. Abraham became the father of God's people. Abraham built an altar to the Lord wherever he was, because he couldn't get away from the word of the Lord.[2]

Questions to Ponder: What does this story say to you? Who was Abraham? What did he do? Name other heroes and heroines in the Bible.

Jane, a four-year-old, listened to the story of Abraham. One day while playing with the cardboard biblical figures, she asked the teacher, "Is this Abraham?"

"No, that is Moses. Let us look for Abraham. Where is Abraham? Do you think he ran away?"

"I think he ran away because he didn't want to move like God wanted him to." Jane had heard!

Children learn the Bible through the adults who know the biblical stories. Tell children your favorite stories and why, recalling the stories you heard as a child, and read the stories again and again. In order to tell or to translate their messages into actions, adults must know the stories. Share with children how the Bible has been meaningful in your own personal life and in the world down through the centuries, for the community of faith has been built around "these stories."

In the Beginning

In the beginning when God created the heavens and the earth. . . . (Gen. 1:1)

In the beginning God created the heavens and the earth." Jesus read the words from the scroll. Then he carefully rolled up the scroll and handed it to his teacher, smiling. "I have learned the words by heart. I can say them without reading," he told the rabbi.

"You have learned well. You are a good student of the Torah (the Jewish Bible)," his teacher replied.

That afternoon Jesus ran all the way home. "Mother, Mother!" he called. "The teacher said I was a good student of the Torah because I learned my verse by memory. I can say it by heart."

Mary hugged her son. "Would you say the words for me?"

Jesus stood before his mother very straight and very still. He spoke the words slowly and in a loud voice. "In the beginning God created the heavens and the earth."

"You remember well," Mary said. "Would you like some bread and cheese?"

"Yes," Jesus nodded his head, "but first I must tell Father the words I have learned. Is he in his carpenter's shop?"

"Yes," Mary replied, as Jesus ran to the carpenter's shop that was beside his home. He opened the door slowly to see if Joseph was alone. Then he asked, "Are you busy, Father?"

"Come in, Jesus. I am not too busy to speak with you. How was school today?"

"The rabbi said I was a good student of the Torah. I memorized the first words."

"Say them for me now, Jesus, as we go for our bread and cheese."

"In the beginning God created the heavens and the earth," Jesus said, opening the door.

As they all sat down at the table, Joseph smiled at Jesus. "You will be a good worker for God. Now, before we eat our bread and cheese, let us all say the words of our faith together."

Mary and Joseph and Jesus said, "In the beginning God created the heavens and the earth."

Questions to Ponder: What words from the Bible do you know by heart? Let's share them together.

Ask the children to say the words with you: "In the beginning God created the heavens and the earth."

To learn by heart is to have something to think about in the dark. Persons in solitary confinement have attested to the importance of learning "by heart." It is a lonely mind that has only its own thoughts for company.

A child once told me that "a poem in my head is like God talking to me." When my son was nine his teacher asked him to choose a poem to memorize "by heart." He chose Robert Frost's "You Come Too." That was the beginning of his years of memorizing. As a student in graduate school, riding his bicycle long distances, he had one eye out for the traffic and the other for the poem he was memorizing.

The little boy wanted to know how long the woman had been a teacher. She sat down, trying to recall how many years it had been since she first entered the classroom. They had all flown past so swiftly. It was at least twenty years since she had first walked into the room and loved each of those children.

The child waited patiently while she remembered.

She smiled as she put her arm around his shoulder and said, "I have been here twenty years."

His eyes grew large. "You must do it *by heart!*"

The child spoke wise words. That is exactly how she did it.

Jesus and the Children

Open a Bible to Mark 10:13-16 and show the boys and girls where the story is written, explaining, "The story I am going to tell you about Jesus is written in the Bible. The Bible is God's storybook."

If appropriate ask children to help you tell the story by acting out the story with you.

*O*ne morning Philip jumped up from his mat on the floor and stretched and smiled. (Jump up, stretch, and smile.)

"Today we are going to see Jesus!" he cried, as he put on his robe (Slip arms into imaginary robe.) and sandals (Lace sandals.), and rolled up his mat. (Roll up mat.) He asked his mother, "What can I do to help get ready?"

"I have packed the lunch," Mother said. "You can sweep the floor."

Philip swept the floor (Sweep.), singing, "We're going to see Jesus! We're going to see Jesus today!" (Sing together.)

Soon Philip was running down the road (Run in place.), shouting, "We're going to see Jesus." (Shout words together.)

Mother could hardly keep up with Philip. Then he suddenly stopped and his mother wondered what was the matter. She ran to Philip. She was worried. (Frown.)

"Philip, what is the matter?"

Philip smiled, showing his mother the wildflowers he had picked. "These are for Jesus to say 'I love you.' (Hold out imaginary flowers.) And these are for you, because I love you too." (Bring out flowers from behind back.)

Mother thanked Philip and then Philip saw the crowd of people on the hillside, but he could not see Jesus. There were so many people, he could not get close. He stood on his tiptoes (Stand on tiptoes.) and told his mother, "I can't see Jesus."

"Perhaps you could wiggle through the crowd and give your gift to Jesus," Mother suggested.

Philip did. (Wiggle through imaginary crowd.) He had almost reached Jesus *when he felt a big hand on his shoulder and heard a loud voice that said, "Jesus is too busy to talk to you now. (Speak in a deep voice.)"*

Philip was afraid of the big man, and was disappointed. He wanted to cry, but he held back the tears.

"Let the children come to me," said a gentle voice. It was Jesus! (Lift head and smile.) Philip ran to him and held out his flowers.

When Jesus took the flowers, he smiled, and then he lifted Philip onto his lap. "God loves children," Jesus said to the crowd of people, and to Philip he said, "And God loves you." (Smile.)

***Questions to Ponder:* Who is Jesus? What did he teach? What did he do? To whom do you belong? (God, family, church)**

Children learn at an affective level rather than a cognitive one. It is more important that a child feel, imagine, and experience than learn "facts." A person may learn a faith vocabulary but his acquaintance with Christ is an affective confrontation with a Person, and for children that person is a Friend.

A family of missionaries in Hong Kong once became very anxious when their small daughter became seriously ill with a type of viral infection. The husband and his wife shared the long vigils at the hospital, waiting with hope in their hearts that their young child would recover. One night when the father was at home with the older daughter, the mother sat at her daughter's bedside, waiting for one small word. Sometime during the early morning hours she heard soft singing, so weak it was almost a sigh. The mother could barely understand the words, but she heard, "Jesus loves me this I know . . . they are weak, but he is strong."

From a very sick little girl came the words of hope and faith, bringing joy to the heart of the weary mother. Trust changes the way we think, the reason we do, and the way we act.

What Does the Lord Require?

What does the LORD require of you but to do justice, and to love kindness, and to walk humbly with your God? (Micah 6:8)

E*veryone is taking bribes, Micah. If we don't, someone else will."*
Micah shook his head. "Are you serious? It is a sin against God."

"Don't play 'goody-goody' with us, Micah. We are taking the money," they replied.

Micah had heard of the corruption in high places but he did not believe God's people would forget their Law. "If this is true, perhaps the other things I have heard are also true," he thought.

Micah walked through the dirty streets of Samaria, littered with garbage and refuse. He grimaced as he saw a dirty beggar pick up a piece of food from the street and greedily eat it. "The people are starving, while those in high places connive and cheat, ignoring the needs of the poor."

Suddenly Micah noticed that he had wandered into the marketplace.

"Your son for a pair of shoes!" said the merchant, rubbing his hands to keep them warm. "Hurry up. Make up your mind. It is cold out here."

An old man held the hand of a small boy. Neither of the two wore shoes. If the merchant had cared enough to look, he would have seen that their feet had turned purple from the cold. They were bleeding as well, from the hard cobblestones. "But he is my son. Give me the shoes and I will be able to work and pay you double," the poor man begged.

"Get out of here until you can return with something more than a worthless promise for a pair of good shoes!" shouted the merchant.

"I have always kept my promises. I may be poor but I am honest." The old man begged the merchant to listen and be merciful. "Be kind and God will bless you."

"As God has blessed you?" mocked the merchant.

The old man began to cry. The merchant raised his arm, as if to strike the poor beggar. Micah could stand it no longer and ran toward the merchant, grabbing his arm. "You have no right to strike."

"The poor have no right . . . " growled the merchant, interrupting Micah. "Who do you think you are?"

Micah ignored the merchant's question and asked, "How much are the shoes?"

The merchant began to laugh until he remembered that a sale was involved. He could laugh after he had his money!

Micah paid the merchant the price he asked and gave the old man the shoes. "Come with me," he said, and took them to a merchant who sold them some bread.

When the old man and his son had eaten, Micah gave them a few coins. "Go in peace and God bless you."

"God bless you, Master."

Micah felt sick inside. He passed the synagogue and saw the people in their fine clothes praying and offering their tithes to the Lord.

"I came to the city to pray but my heart is too sad." Micah glanced again at the congregation gathered together, unaware of the sick, lonely, and poor people outside. "He has showed you, O man, what is good; and what does the Lord require of you?"

Then, as if to answer his own question, Micah continued, "But to do justice, and to love kindness, and to walk humbly with your God."

No one heard the words Micah spoke that day. He returned to his home and wrote what he had seen and heard and felt.

Micah never forgot that day in the city. For the rest of his life he worked for and preached for justice for all people, rich and poor, young and old, wise and unlearned, as he walked humbly with his Lord.

Questions to Ponder: **What does this story say to you? Where do you see injustice? What can we do? What are we doing?**

The Bible is the story of a people encountering God in their daily living, and the story of their response. The Bible is a "never-ending story." It teaches us to hope and cope. It gives us a vision and a promise by which to live: the presence of God here and now.

The Bible is a book of faith about God, the living Jesus and the Christ of faith, and the Holy Spirit, about a world that is "flat," but only in shape on a globe, for in reality this world is round and full of mystery and meaning. We tell biblical stories to children so they may enter that "world" with us, hear it speak in its own language, and participate in it imaginatively, as our story.

Noah and the Flood

Noah found favor in the sight of the LORD. (Gen. 6:8)

No one enjoyed a story more than Amos. After a long, hot day walking across the desert, looking for water for their sheep and goats, Amos and his family would put up their tents, roast a goat, and sit around the fire eating cheese and bread and meat. As soon as the sun left the sky, the hot, dusty day turned cold and dry.

Amos wrapped his cloak around him as Grandfather stirred the fire. The flames rose higher and Amos moved closer to watch the pictures that formed in the fire. They were blue, red, and yellow flames, reminding Amos of the rainbow he had seen in the sky that day.

One by one the family gathered around the flames of the fire. "Grandfather, what is a rainbow? Tell us a story," Amos suggested, eagerly looking forward to this time.

Grandfather smiled as he seated himself, warming his hands at the fire and speaking slowly as he recalled the story of their forefather of the faith:

His name was Noah, which means "comfort," Grandfather began. . . .

In a time that never was and always is, God called to Noah one day, but Noah was drawing pictures for his granddaughter in the sand and did not hear God's call.

"Noah," God called again. But just as God called, Esther, Noah's granddaughter, whispered in his ear, "I love you, Grandpa," and Noah did not hear God speaking.

"Noah!" God called the third time. "Noah, listen to me. I . . . "

"God? You called?" Noah asked, listening.

"Noah, what is the matter with the people on Earth? Why don't they hear me?"

"I don't know, God," said Noah, shaking his head.

"Noah, I made them a good world to live in. They should be happy, but they are instead destroying my Earth, their home." This time God did not wait for Noah to reply. "I want you to do something for me. It will be difficult, but it is for the good of all people. Will you do it, Noah?"

Noah hesitated, not knowing what God might ask of him. Yet Noah knew God loved him and wanted the best for him and for all people and replied, "Yes! Lord. What is it?"

"I want you to build an ark, a house that floats." Then God told Noah how big the boat should be.

"That big? I don't know if I can find that much wood. Why a boat that big would take me and my sons at least a year to build!"

Now God was silent. So Noah was too, and the next day Noah found enough wood to build the ark. "Old neighbor, sell me all the wood you have. I am going to build a house that will float. There is going to be a flood, waters will pour from the sky."

The neighbor laughed and laughed. "Old Noah, have you lost your senses? Look at the sky. Not a single dark cloud!" Then he thought. "I will sell you the wood," he said, and charged Noah three times as much as it was worth, for Noah's neighbors were greedy.

When he took the money, he laughed and laughed, and Noah took the wood and carried it home.

"Old friend," he called, seeing how heavy the wood was. "Help me carry home this wood. I am going to build a house that will float. There is going to be a flood, waters will pour from the sky."

The old friend laughed. "Old Noah, you can't be serious. We haven't had rain for months and this is not the rainy season." But when he saw that Noah was serious, he added, "I will help you, if you pay me."

40

When he took the money, he laughed and laughed, and Noah began to build the ark. Then he called to his sons, "I need your help."

"I'm busy, Father," said one of them.

"I don't feel very well," said another.

"I'm tired," said still another.

The boys hated to work. Noah looked at his sons and became angry. He picked up his hammer and began to work. "Ouch!" he screamed suddenly. The hammer had hit his finger and it puffed up like a balloon. Now both his hand and his feelings were hurt. He wondered if he had really heard God right. Perhaps he had misunderstood.

As his children watched Noah build, one of them picked up a piece of wood and carried it to his father. The second picked up a hammer and began to pound, and soon the whole family was helping. With everyone working together, the boat was finished.

Still there was no flood. Only the Voice. "Noah, take two of every animal and place them in the boat."

"What?" asked Noah.

"You heard me," God said.

And when the animals were in the boat and Noah shut the door, it began to rain and rain and rain, just as God had said. There was a flood.

Forty days and forty nights the boat floated on the water. Then one day it landed on dry land. Noah and his family and the animals all left the boat, and in their joy and relief to be on land, they knelt on the ground and thanked God.

Noah waited to hear God speak, as God had before, but now there was no Voice. "Father, look!" his son exclaimed, pointing to the clear sky above. Across the heavens there appeared a beautiful, multicolored rainbow, stretching from earth to sky.

And deep in Noah's heart he heard the words, "I will be with you always." Noah smiled, knowing God has many different ways of speaking.

Questions to Ponder: What does this story say to you? What does a rainbow mean? Who tells you stories? Who tells you Bible stories? If you were on a boat for forty days and nights, what would you miss most?

Often we ask, "Why do we want to tell this parable based on a Bible story? What does it convey to children about God? About the Bible?

41

All children have experiences and feelings. They experience love and law, fear and envy and rejection, satisfaction and disappointment. They are curious and look for relationships among people and things.

The people in the Bible are like you and me, with some of the same thoughts and feelings, and God loved and worked through them, as God loves and works through us. What is important in the child's encounter with the Bible is that the story has personal relevance.

The following activities are suggested for engaging children in the story of Noah:

1. Ask children to identify with one animal. Interview them as a "television reporter," by asking: "I understand you were on the boat with Noah. Would you please tell our audience what it was like. How did you feel during those days and nights on the boat? Did you make new friends? What did you miss most? What impressed you most about the trip? What would you like us to remember from your story?" Others may wish to ask questions, as well.

2. With older children discuss the symbolism of the story: What does this story say to you? Have you ever experienced a storm or flood, or some other scary situation, in your life? Where was God? What do you think is the meaning of the story? What does the rainbow represent for you?

3. Draw a mural of Noah's ark. Brainstorm a title for the mural.

4. Cut pictures from magazines or draw animals and glue pieces of flannel or felt to the back of each picture for use in telling the story on a feltboard. Ask the children to tell the story, as they recall it.

Seeds

And he told them many things in parables, saying: "Listen! A sower went out to sow." (Matt. 13:3)

Listen my children and give heed,
A sower set out to sow his seed
On a warm and sunny day.
Packing his sack with

Seeds to sow,
The sower threw out his seeds to grow,
And some fell along the way.
Hungry birds eager for their feed,
Flew down to devour every seed
'Till the path was smooth and bare.
Some of the seeds fell on a stone
And shriveled up when the warm sun shown,
So no one knew they were there.
Those that fell in the thorns and weeds
Were choked and destroyed, but the seeds
That fell in the rich, wet ground
Grew from the sunshine and the rain
Into the ripened golden grain,
Filling fields for miles around.
He who has ears then let him hear,
For Jesus was speaking to those near
In a way they'd understand.
People who love and do good deeds,
Whose faith is in God are like the seeds
That grew in the way God planned.[3]

Invite the children to participate in the retelling of the story below by performing the motions.

Reader: "Listen!"

Group: (Cup hand behind ear. Look expectant.)

Reader: A farmer went out to sow his seed.

Group: (Make large swinging movements with right arm. Take long steps to the swinging movement. Be sure there is enough room.)

Reader: As he was scattering the seed, some fell along the path.

Group: (One half of children are the seeds, while the other half are birds flying around the seeds.)

Reader: The birds came and ate them up. Some fell on rocky places, where there was no soil. The seed sprang up quickly.

Group: ("Seeds" jump up, moving around the room.)

Reader: But when the sun came up, the plants were scorched, and they withered because they had no root.

(One person pretending to be the sun steps regally among the seeds, chest, shoulders, and head thrown back and walking with slow, large, sweeping arm movements. The "seeds" droop with lower heads, shoulders forward, and drop to the floor as limp ragdolls.)

Reader: Other seed fell among thorns, which grew up and choked the plants, so that they did not bear grain.

("Seeds" slowly lift heads, shoulders, bodies to full height. "Thorns" will "choke" the "seeds." Seeds struggle, slowly "expire," and lie on the floor.)

Reader: Still other seed fell on good soil. They came up, grew and produced a crop, multiplying thirty, sixty, or even a hundred times."

("Seeds" slowly, with strong movements, raise heads, bodies, and arms. Stand up and dance, moving freely without touching one another.)

Questions to Ponder: **Think of the wonder of a seed. There is life inside, waiting for the right moment to explode into what it was meant to be, but it needs something. What does it need? (Perhaps good soil, or the nourishment of sunshine and rain.) As a person what do you need? What robs you of your growth? What if you had no food? no water? no place to live? God's aim and desire is for food, water, home, education, and love for everyone, and where this happens, there is the "kingdom of God" on earth. How did Jesus teach the kingdom of God? What does this story say about the kingdom of God? How do you experience the kingdom of God?**

Parables invite us to struggle with their meaning, as Jacob struggled with the angel until he received the blessing. Symbols and stories point to, suggest, and describe what is undefinable. A story can express a complex fact not yet understood with the mind.

Confronting the parable is being confronted *by* the parable, and interpreting its meaning for oneself releases within the hearer an intense sort of spiritual activity that is not possible through a didactic approach with a single meaning that we are told.

The biblical stories are never fully understood because we never stop discovering new meaning. Layer on layer with truth at the center, the stories give us our sense of identity and our sense of mission.

44

Solomon's Dream

At Gibeon the Lord *appeared to Solomon in a dream by night; and God said, "Ask what I should give you." (1 Kings 3:5)*

Talk together about dreams and ask the children to picture the story as you tell it:

Long ago there lived a king who was very, very wise. One night, while he was sleeping, the Lord appeared to him in a dream and said to him, "Ask what I should give you."

King Solomon thanked God for the love God had given to his father, King David. Now as king, taking his father's place, Solomon said to God, "I am only a little child; I do not know how to go out or come in."

He was being humble before God, his Creator and Lord. "Give your servant, therefore, an understanding mind to rule your people; able to decide [discern] between good and evil."

God was pleased because Solomon did not ask for a long life or riches, but for understanding. Solomon wanted to know what God wanted for his people. He wanted to do God's will. So God answered his prayer and made Solomon the wisest of all kings.

Questions to Ponder: If God said you could ask for anything you wanted, for what would you ask? For what did Solomon ask? How did God answer Solomon's request? When Jesus taught his friends to pray, he said, "Say, 'Your (speaking to God) will be done.' " This was Jesus' prayer, as well.

Neither Solomon nor Jesus prayed for things for themselves but trusted God and asked for good for others and for God's greater future, which Jesus called "The Kingdom of God."

In the Bible we read the stories of many persons who opened themselves to God and heard God speak to them in dreams or visions. Through their dreams they learned to trust God. We too can trust God because we know God is trustworthy through God's plan for all people. God's plan is love through Jesus Christ and God wants us to love and trust that nothing can separate us from God's love.

Dreams can be one of the ways God reveals. The biblical writers understood dreams as a way that God revealed [spoke] to men and women. To dream is to sleep, to let go of conscious thinking and will and "drop down into" or "rise up to," metaphors for sensing a different reality from daytime wakefulness. The whole of reality cannot be contained or experienced in the waking hours alone. Today many modern "healers" speak of dreams as a voice of inner truth. Dreams are the way we story our lives in sleep.

The Good Bird 6.10.18

Read aloud from your Bible Luke 10:30-37 before you tell the story.

There was once a small fish. The fish lived in the water and played in the waves and swam with the other fish. But this fish, named Franklin, was adventurous and though small, liked to leave the others and look for beautiful seashells at the bottom of the ocean.

"Look where you're going!" cried a school of fish that Franklin ran into without realizing it. They were swimming in one direction, and Franklin was swimming in the opposite direction.

There were many things to see in the ocean. Franklin visited the deepest, darkest places and was not frightened.

Franklin learned where to hide in order to escape the jaws and stomachs of the bigger fish, for Franklin was a very small fish.

Because Franklin was small he could dart in and out of pink and yellow coral reefs. He could admire the beautiful orange and green fins of the sea creatures and explore their caves and castles.

One day Franklin's adventuring took him into a small cove. Here the water was shallow and he could swim close to the land.

On the sand, Franklin saw a mermaid with long black moss hair, surrounded by seashells of all sizes and shapes. He didn't realize that this was only a beach towel.

Being curious, he swam to where the water and shore met. He heard the loud roar of the sea monster's motor and felt the waves it created. One wave after another slammed against the small fish.

Before Franklin knew what had happened, he lay on the land in pain from the beating of the waves.

Half dead, he panted for life.

Who would help him return to the water?

Now by chance a mother, unpacking her picnic basket, saw the helpless fish. "People care. Maybe the mother will help me," Franklin thought.

But the mother returned to unpacking the picnic basket, while the sun dried Franklin's gills and it became harder and harder to breathe.

A child with a sandbucket, hearing his mother call, ran toward the small fish and seeing him, stopped to look. Franklin hoped.

46

"Alan!" the child heard the call again.

"Coming!" he cried, running through the sand, spraying it over the small fish lying helplessly on the sand, abandoned.

And then the greatest danger of all!

Franklin could see the enemy in the distance, becoming larger and larger. When the big bird swooped down to grab Franklin in its beak, all hope left the small fish.

"I wonder how far he will take me to be lunch for his children?" Franklin thought, as the bird lifted him from the land.

But the Good Bird opened its beak and gently dropped Franklin into the cool, wet water he called home.

Questions to Ponder: How would you have felt if you were Franklin? What would you have done if you saw Franklin on the beach? How does this story remind you of Jesus' story?

The first creation story tells us of God's will that we care for the creatures of the earth. Why didn't the mother or child help the fish?

Stories can ignite the imagination. They suggest possibility, "If I had been the child and saw the fish, I would have . . . " and identification, "If I had been the fish . . . "

Stories have that power because they speak to the heart as well as the head. They provide an intuitive way of knowing. The soul prefers imagination over reason.

Sometimes children (and adults) feel God has abandoned, abused, or judged them and lose trust and hope, as the man on the road to Jericho, or as the small fish. Their deepest fear is about to happen and where is God now?

This story, however, says that we are wrong. Ours is a gracious, generous God. The Samaritan or the bird is God in disguise, the loving, compassionate One. When we love we reveal God's love.

The Rich Young Man

Jesus looked at him with love. "You need to do one thing more," he said. "Sell all that you have and give it to the poor and you will have riches in heaven. Then come and follow me." (based on Luke 18:18-30)

*W*hen one of the members of a leading family heard this he became very sad and went away sorrowing.

Those who heard Jesus' words asked, "Who then can be saved?"

Jesus replied, "With God all things are possible."

The rich, young man who had asked Jesus the question was no longer young. As his age increased so did his riches, and his disease. One night, when he was old, sitting in his magnificent home, surrounded by thick Oriental carpets, pearl-inlaid furniture, heavy brocaded curtains, and luxurious foods, his discomfort grew into despair and he recalled the day he had encountered the wandering preacher, the one some said was "the Son of God." That day he had asked him how he could inherit eternal life, but Jesus' reply had been too demanding, too unreasonable, too unrealistic. What did this poor preacher know about money? The old man remembered now how he had felt great sorrow as he left Jesus. Today he was even richer than he had been then. But if he was so rich, why was he not happy? In this mood he fell asleep and in his dream he again encountered Jesus.

Once more Jesus looked at him with love. "Have you used God's gifts well?" he asked.

"I have tithed. I have given one-tenth of my riches to the poor," the old man replied.

"You have given what was not yours."

"No! No! I have only given what belonged to me. I have never robbed nor cheated anyone," he protested.

"What you have is not yours," Jesus replied quietly. "What you have belongs to them. Is it better to have wealth or to give it away? What riches do you have in heaven? Sell all that you have and give it to the poor and then come and follow me."

The words Jesus spoke were the same words he had said long ago. Again the man's heart was strangely moved. Was it possible that he was being given a second chance?

"But, Master, I am too old to follow you now." Again the man was full of sorrow. It was too late. If only he had listened to Jesus the first time!

There was silence. The silence was as a wall between them, a wall between the old man and God, and he began to cry. If only it were possible to have a second chance!

Jesus spoke through the silence and as he spoke the wall crumbled. "With God all things are possible," he said.

The old man awoke from his sleep. He looked at his thick, rich carpets, his expensive curtains, his priceless furniture and slowly lifted himself to his feet.

That day, when he had sold all that he had and given it to the poor, he felt richer than he had ever been before, for now he was filled and surrounded by God.

Questions to Ponder: **This story is not in the Bible. Do you think it is possible? What does the story say to you? Was Jesus rich or poor?**

The Bible portrays human existence in all its possibility: its depth and height, our drives and dreams, our prides and passions, revenges and regrets.

Children learn from the words adults use. They also learn from their attitudes, and when the Bible and its stories are important to the family at home and the family at church, they become interested in them. We use the Bible with children to acquaint them with their religious heritage and the stories of "our people," our forebears in the faith. Above all, we use the Bible to help them know God's love for them as special, unique persons. They learn that love as we live the Bible's message with our lives in relationship. For even more than hearing words from the Bible, children learn the biblical truths from the relationships they experience with the people who know and communicate God's words with their lives.

The Second Mile

Based on Matthew 5:39-41.

*I*f someone slaps you on the face, turn the other side of your face so he can slap that side as well."

Caleb and Jonah began to laugh. "That's a good joke, Timothy."

"I'm not joking. That is what Jesus said and he meant it. I heard him myself."

"I don't get it," said Caleb.

"It's a way to show love," said Timothy.

"It seems stupid to me," Caleb continued. "Why, the person who hit you would think that you were a coward . . . or stupid."

The boys continued to talk as they walked to the village.

"Hey, you, boy, come here," shouted a voice with a Roman accent.

It was a Roman soldier. The Romans ruled Timothy's country. They were harsh and cruel and the conquered people hated them.

"Someday," Timothy thought, "we will be free of these Roman conquerors!"

"You, the short one, come here!" the Roman repeated.

The boys looked at each other to see who was the shortest. Timothy stepped forward. "Pick up this bag, boy, and follow me."

Caleb and Jonah backed away slowly and disappeared. Timothy picked up the bag. He walked as far behind the Roman soldier as possible, because he did not want to be near someone he hated.

It was a long walk and the bag was heavy. As the sun became hotter, the walk longer, the bag became heavier. The soldier looked at Timothy and offered him some of his water to drink. Timothy shook his head. He would not touch anything Roman that he was not ordered to touch.

In order to forget his tired feet and sore arms, Timothy thought about the previous day, when he had heard Jesus teaching the people on the hillside. He heard his words now. "If anyone forces you to go one mile, go with him two."

Timothy continued to walk behind the soldier. Suddenly, he did not like these teachings of Jesus. He agreed with Caleb and Jonah. They didn't make sense and they were hard to follow.

"Stop here," the soldier said, speaking sharply to disguise his concern for the tired boy.

Timothy continued to walk, for he knew the city was yet another mile away.

"I said to stop here. You are finished. I don't need you any longer."

Timothy continued to walk.

"Do you hear me?" The soldier's concern had changed to anger because the boy would not listen. He became so angry he ran up to Timothy and slapped him across the face.

Timothy's eyes flashed. He clenched his fists. His heart beat faster. Then he turned his other cheek toward the Roman for him to strike.

The soldier stared at Timothy. Timothy picked up the bag and began to walk again.

"Who are you?" the soldier asked, keeping in step with the pace of Timothy.

Before Timothy could think, the words leaped out. "A follower of Jesus," he replied. Suddenly Timothy sighed. Yes, he had just followed Jesus' teachings.

"I'm sorry," said the Roman, seeing Timothy shift the heavy bag. "Let me carry it the rest of the way."

"No, I will finish my job . . . gladly," Timothy said, for now he knew who he was, and when Timothy told Jonah and Caleb what had happened, Caleb said, "Good for you, Timothy, for making that Roman feel bad."

Timothy was surprised at his reply. "I didn't want to make him feel bad, Caleb. I even forgot that I hated him. Jesus was right after all."

Questions to Ponder: **Have you ever "turned the other cheek" or "walked the second mile"? What does that mean? Have you ever hated anyone? How did it make you feel? What does Jesus teach us?**

Jesus taught through his actions and his words, leading persons to make judgments, decisions, and commitments, to redeem and transform this world, for redemption and transformation are within this world.

God's mode of revelation is personal, the Person of Christ and God incarnate in others. Jesus was the Incarnation of God's living word, God's word of surprise and miracle, for the biggest surprise and miracle of all was that Jesus, who lived and died a parable teller, arose from death the Parable of God.

♡

To See and Walk

Then some people came, bringing to [Jesus] a paralyzed man, carried by four of them. (Mark 2:3)

If only I could see . . . " said the blind man, feeling his way along the road with a stick in his hand. His stick served as his eyes.

"Where are you going?" cried a voice by the side of the road.

"I am going to the next village to visit my mother, for she is ill," the blind man replied to the stranger. "But soon it will be dark!"

"What does that matter to you?" asked the lame man at the side of the road, resting because of his lameness. "You cannot see anyway."

"Yes, but in the dark robbers roam the countryside. I must be in the village before dark, but it is slow to walk without seeing."

"Talk about slow. You cannot see me, I know, but I am lame. I too am going to the village ahead, but because I am lame, it is slow to walk."

The blind man sat down beside the lame man and they talked of their illnesses.

"Because I cannot see, I am cut off from others," the blind man complained.

"Because I cannot walk, I am cut off from others," the lame man complained.

As they complained and felt sorry for themselves, the sun slowly descended in the sky.

"Soon it will be dark. I wish I could walk."

The blind man was silent. He had stopped complaining and was listening, thinking, and remembering.

"I remember hearing a story about four friends who brought their lame friend to the man called Jesus, who healed him," the blind man spoke at last.

"Where is this man Jesus? Will he help us?"

"He was killed, but his friends say he is still with them, reminding them that God's power is with us all, even the ill."

"Not the lame . . . "

Suddenly the blind man stood up and shouted, "Yes, with the lame and the blind!"

"What are you talking about? Have you lost your mind?"

"No, I have just found it. As the four friends carried their lame friend, I will carry you. God empowers us all. I will be your feet and you will be my eyes. Together we will walk to the village before dark!"

And so it was . . .

Questions to Ponder: What does it mean to "lose your mind"? What did the blind man mean "I have found it"? How did the two men get to the village before dark? Have you ever needed someone to help you? Has anyone ever needed your help? How can Bible stories become our "friends" to help us?

Christianity calls us both to "see" and "walk" (to do). *Together* we can become whole.

The Bible "befriends" us by empowering us through its stories of trust in God's love and power.

Zacchaeus

Based on Luke 19:1-10.

*O*ne morning the children and I put on our "magic flying shoes," used our imaginations, and flew to a country far away and long ago, where Jesus used to live.

When we "landed," we took off our shoes immediately so that we would not accidentally fly away again, but even more important, so that we could feel the soft, warm sand of Palestine.

Sometimes we stubbed our toes on stones. There are many stones in Palestine! That is why Jesus wore sandals.

"What shall we do?" I asked. Some of the children suggested singing. Some said, "We can walk."

We walked together. Some of us walked with a partner. Some ran ahead to pick wildflowers. Some wandered and wondered, taking time, each one at his or her own pace.

Then one of the teachers saw a man climbing a tree. "Did you see that?" she asked the boys and girls who stopped to watch the man, because it is not too often we see grown-ups climbing trees. "I wonder why he is climbing the tree?" the teacher asked aloud.

"To see!" someone cried.

"Of course. I wonder what he wants to see? I wonder what he will see?"

"Clouds!" Karen suggested, for she had recently been on a picnic with her family and they had watched the clouds together.

"Yes, clouds," agreed the teacher. "I wonder what else we would see if we were high up in a tree?"

"Birds!" shouted some of the children. "Airplanes. Grass. People." said others.

"Let's ask the man in the tree!" said William.

The man answered, "I wanted to see Jesus. Because I am small, too small to see in a crowd of people, I thought and thought, 'What can I do?' Then I had an idea. 'I will climb a tree so I can see!' "

No one helped Zacchaeus because he had cheated them out of their money. No one liked Zacchaeus. So Zacchaeus felt little "inside" as well as out.

Zacchaeus (that was the little man's name) climbed the tree to see Jesus. Jesus saw Zacchaeus, too. "Zacchaeus," Jesus called, "come down. Let us go to your house and talk."

We followed Jesus.

After the long walk, we were tired and sat down to rest while Jesus went inside Zacchaeus's house to talk.

"I wonder what they are doing? I wonder what they are eating? I wonder what they are talking about?" We all wondered together.

"The door is opening. Jesus is coming out. What is he saying to Zacchaeus? Let's listen," the teacher suggested.

In the silence we heard the words together. "I am your friend," Jesus said. "God loves you."

Together, each of us said, "God loves (our own name)," before we raced for our magic shoes, for it was time to fly home!

If you prefer, substitute the following poem:

Zacchaeus
Zacchaeus was a little man
Who climbed into a tree
And you and I know why because
Sometimes we cannot see.
Zacchaeus heard that Jesus was
A wise and loving man
Who showed God's love and care, forgave,
And taught God's loving plan.
I like to hear how Jesus said,
"Come down, I've come to you,
To show you how to love and care."
I think he means me, too.

Questions to Ponder: **If you had met Zacchaeus before Zacchaeus met Jesus, do you think you would have liked him? What does it mean that Zacchaeus felt little "inside"? Are there people you do not like? What was Zacchaeus's problem? Did Jesus know this? How did Jesus help Zacchaeus? Sometimes we, like Zacchaeus, do things people do not like. How does Jesus help you be the person others like? How can we help the people we do not like?**

This story is in the Bible. (Read Luke 19:1-10 aloud, holding the Bible.)

Invite the children (and congregation) to do a guided faith meditation:

Take three deep breaths and be silent within yourself. Rest a second and then walk slowly down a dusty road. You have cheated someone by not being loving or by not forgiving or by taking something from them they did not want to give, or by doing something to them that hurt them. Perhaps you have cheated yourself someway, or maybe you have cheated God. Think what that might be. (Pause.) Ask yourself, "What can I do?" (Pause.)

Your questions and thoughts are interrupted by loud shouts. "Jesus is coming! Jesus, the Son of God, is here!"

"Maybe this Jesus can help me," you think and look around. A large crowd of people has gathered. They push and shove you. You cannot see. You cannot breathe. You feel too small to be noticed by Jesus. Again you think, "What can I do?" (Pause.)

You see a tree and quickly climb it. It feels good to take the initiative for yourself. As you sit in the tree, you wait and watch and listen to Jesus telling the people, "God loves you. God forgives you. You must love and forgive others."

You remember your problem and begin to worry again and are sorry, until you hear Jesus say, "I want to be with you today."

"Me?" Surprised but pleased, you climb down the tree and take Jesus to your home, into your inner heart.

With Jesus beside you, you feel God's love. You give your problem to God and feel his acceptance and forgiveness. You confess to the person you have wronged, whether it is yourself, another, or God. When you are ready, open your eyes and return to this place.

Zacchaeus, being small and eager to see what kind of man Jesus was, climbed a tree to discover Jesus was "Lord."

Zacchaeus experienced transformation and shared his gifts with the poor. He may not have grown physically, but he did grow spiritually.

"You're big. I'm small. Take care of me." This reminds us of the Breton's prayer: "Please God take care of me. My boat is so small and the waves are so high."

Baal Shem taught his followers to fight sadness and "smallness" with joy: "The man who looks only at himself cannot but sink into despair, yet as soon as he opens his eyes to the creation about him, he will know joy."

The Bible was written long ago and far away. Young children, however, are here and now people. Our challenge, therefore, is to combine their love of stories and their desire to move, by involving them in participating in the story through the imagination.

Inasmuch

"And the king will answer them, 'Truly I tell you, just as you did it to one of the least of these who are members of my family, you did it to me.' "
(Matt. 25:40)

> If I had lived when Jesus lived, I'd ask him in to tea
> And give him gifts and listen to the stories he told me.
> He never would be lonely and he never would be cold,
> For I would keep him company, and then when I was old,
> I'd bring my children unto him. But Jesus said, "You see,
> Inasmuch as you love others, you show your love for me."

Questions to Ponder: What would you do if Jesus came to visit you? (Read the Bible verse above.) What do those words mean to you?

The best predictor of a child's performance of love and sharing is the love and learning in the child's home with which the child is nurtured.

Parents who trust themselves and their children provide the most important step in growing: trust. Trust in God is nurtured by prayer and sustained by the life of the imagination. We grow from the inside out. Growth is part of God's plan for life.

When children learn trust (growing from inside out), they develop in their unique ways.

Children: Enjoying "Me!"

Children enjoy stories. Through stories they learn they are important to God and to one another. The Bible is the story of encounters between God and God's people, and the people's responses.

A lonely television set sat in the classroom and was never turned on. A stranger, seeing the unused television, was shocked. "Why don't you use your television?" he asked the children.

They simply replied, "We have a storyteller."

"But the television tells thousands of stories," he continued.

"Yes," they agreed, "but the storyteller knows us."

I walked into the church one Sunday morning and was warmly greeted by the man at the door who shook my hand. Beside me, five-year-old Charles put out his hand, as he had been taught and as he had seen me do, but the man did not look down to see his gesture, and Charles quickly withdrew his hand.

We tell stories to children to give them special attention because so often we ignore them. Jesus taught us otherwise and welcomed the children!

A Very Special Friend

The fruit of the Spirit is love, joy, peace, patience, kindness, generosity, faithfulness, gentleness, and self-control. (Gal. 5:22)

*T*o most people, Nero was only a stuffed toy animal, a furry black dog.

To Lauren, Nero was her special friend.

"Nero told me not to hit," Lauren explained to her teacher, when she walked away from the fighting children.

"Nero is only a toy," said her teacher.

When Lauren's brother Bill suggested they sample Mother's freshly baked cookies she had made for her sick friend, Lauren said, "Nero told me not to."

"Aw, Nero's only a toy. He can't talk," said her brother.

When Lauren saw old Mrs. Gray coming down the sidewalk, carrying a heavy bag of groceries, she ran to help her.

"Thank you, Lauren. Come inside for a treat," Mrs. Gray invited Lauren. As they drank the cold milk and ate the chocolate cookies, Mrs. Gray said, "It was kind of you to help me. What made you do it?"

"Nero told me to." Lauren introduced Mrs. Gray to Nero, for Nero and Lauren were always together.

Mrs. Gray laughed. "What an imagination! A talking toy dog!"

To most people, Nero was only a stuffed toy animal but to Lauren, Nero was a special friend. Because of Nero, Lauren was never lonely or afraid. Nero was her friend.

At breakfast Father shook his head. "This isn't good. Lauren acts as if that toy were real! You have to talk to her," he said to his wife.

"Nero, which you call a 'toy,' has taught our daughter to use her imagination and good common sense rather than use violence, to be honest, and to care for and help others. Who are we to say that Nero isn't 'real'!"

To most people, Nero was only a stuffed toy animal but to Lauren, Nero was a very special friend.

Questions to Ponder: Who is your "very special friend"?

If you wish to have a "blessing of the animals," ask the children to bring their "very special friend" to worship today. In a time of playing with violent toys, such "friends" deserve blessing.

Children use their imaginations to provide themselves with helpful companions. Animals real or stuffed, rocks, and toys become objects with personalities to which children talk and relate.

Recent studies show that children with such companions are less lonely, better able to adjust to traumatic situations, have more patience, persistence, and concentration, and are more able to empathize with others. The child's needs for love, affection, companionship, and adventure can be fulfilled through the imagination.

A study in London of 702 children indicated that 16 percent of the three-year-olds who used a stuffed toy or special blanket were the better for it. Children using such comforters were slightly more independent than nonusers and they slept better and their nights were more cheerful.

Books

Do not be conformed to this world, but be transformed by the renewing of your minds. (Rom. 12:2)

I often take my storybooks
And sit upon the stairs,
Where there are birds and elephants,
And kangaroos and bears
That tell me all about the jungle and the zoo,
The tigers, and the lions,
Giraffes, and funny monkeys too.
For books are very special
In a special sort of way.
I always listen carefully
To what they have to say.
Sometimes the planes and trains will rumble 'cross the stairs,
Racing cars and boats that sail, and horses matched in pairs,
And spaceships shiny bright and new to take me to the moon,
So I can sit here on the stairs long into afternoon.
And when it's late and time for bed,
And Mother calls to me,
I take my storybooks to her and listen quietly
To stories I have never heard
And friends I've never met,
Yet I would know most anywhere . . . from books . . .
For books are very special
In a special sort of way.
That's why I listen carefully
To what they have to say!

Questions to Ponder: **What is your favorite book (or story)? Who reads to you?**

Books and stories that absorb the child's interest may transform their thoughts and feelings. Books feed the mind and soul, for when a child is engaged with a book or story, time stands still. Children who enjoy stories and books can learn to live with silence and solitude in a very noisy, competitive world.

Reading now as children will also help them as young people when they face negative peer pressure. Reading helps all of us transform our need for developing self-esteem from the opinions of others to our opinions. We need friends, of course, and books and stories can help us choose the friends we need.

Reading aloud together can help transform a situation by renewing (refreshing, changing) our thoughts and feelings.

A Boy and His Wish

"Ask, and it will be given you." (Luke 11:9a)

> A piece of wood
> a line
> a kitchen knife
> and time
>   +
> a hidden place
> alone
> a bit of string
> a stone
>   +
> a brook or stream
> a wish
> and soon, perhaps
> a fish.

Questions to Ponder: What did the boy wish for? Do you have wants and wishes? What would you like now? Do you always get what you ask for or want?

Jesus said, "Ask, and it will be given you." On the one hand no one can read your mind. So ask, when you are sad or angry or have a question. A response will be given you . . . well, not always. I think Jesus knew that, for in the Garden before his death he asked God to help him not die. Then Jesus added, "Nevertheless, your will, God, be done." Jesus knew that God knew best.

The Cook and the Cake

Whoever walks in integrity walks securely,
*   but whoever follows perverse ways will be found out. (Prov. 10:9)*

59

A cook had been a faithful worker for many years. One day her mistress said, "I want you to make the finest, most delicious cake you've ever made. Do not spare the expense, for I will pay whatever it costs."

The cook thought of the many years she had worked for this woman and she remembered too that it was a special day, her birthday, and believing she deserved something, she thought, "I will make a cheap cake and keep the difference in cost. No one will ever know."

The cook bought cheaper and fewer ingredients and put the rest of the money in her pocket.

While the cake was in the oven her mistress returned home. "Happy Birthday!" she said. "The cake you have just made is your own. I hope you will enjoy it."

Questions to Ponder: **What did that story say to you? After my sons began arguing about who took the biggest piece of cake, we would have one son cut the pieces and the other choose first. What happens in your family concerning sharing?**

> We have shaped our world from blocks.
> "This is yours." "This is mine."
> This is the beginning of sharing.
> And the end?
> "This is ours."

When children know the joy and security of possession, of owning something of their own, it is easier to share with others. One day when I was visiting the beach with three kindergartners, I saw a toddler on a rubber raft and heard him suddenly cry. Thinking my friends had taken the raft from the little one or that the child had fallen off it, I ran to the pool in time to hear the father, with the small child in his arms, say, "It's all right, he has to learn to share!"

Imagine yourself in the toddler's place, having fun on a raft, minding your own business, when along come three huge children who surround you, and being small and unsure, you cry out for safety to the one you count on for security, only to have your joy, your object of pleasure, taken from you for no good reason, and given to them. Why? What kind of a world is this? Where is my safety, joy, comfort? What confusion!

In a loving environment children adapt, but sharing and giving up possessions is a lifelong learning process. Even adults have problems learning this. Sharing comes out of good feelings from experienced love and wanting to please. With patience, time, and experience children learn its importance.

Safety in the Dark

"Do not let your hearts be troubled, and do not let them be afraid."
(John 14:27c)

Of everything in the house the stairs were the most frightening. As she ran up the stairs she shivered because she never knew what would be at the top of the stairs. Nor did she ever question why she ran up the stairs in the dark.

Quickly she undressed. Bed, blanket, and sheet over her head meant safety. She never questioned, when she was young, why she was afraid of the dark or why a blanket or sheet covering her kept her safe. She only knew that it did.

She did know that there were other children who did not go to bed in the dark and were not alone, for she lived beside a family of seven and envied them, as she read her books, a solitary child, an "only" child, for that was her other safety in the dark . . . stories.

Books introduced her to happy places, and as she grew, to darker places as well. And years and years later, as a grandmother reading to her grandchild in the gathering dark, she remembered with gratitude how her fear of the dark had become a love for the dark, for its soft sounds, its tender touch, its restful dreams, and its time to read of people like and unlike herself, away from the world of noise and people-in-skin.

She remembered other times in the dark as a child, of walking alone at night, and thinking one very large tree was trying to grab her. Years later trees and imagination became her close friends.

Returning home in the dark from the Christmas pageant at church on Christmas Eve, she found the door to the living room tightly closed, for Santa had come, and one must not interrupt Santa's gift-giving. Outside the dark night was alive with snow and stars. Inside it was alive with anticipation.

In the night when it is dark is a good time to think about being with God. If we are afraid, it is hard to go to sleep. If we are with God, we can let go of our fear. The Bible tells about Jesus stilling a storm. In the dark we can spend time thanking God for the light of the stars and moon and God's good plan of love. We can think of a word or phrase to repeat over and over, such as "Thank you, God, for being near," or hear the words Jesus said to his friends, "Do not let your hearts be troubled, and do not let them be afraid."

Jesus said that he came to help those in need. It is when we are aware of our need or fear that we seek help.

Questions to Ponder: **What do you do when you are afraid in the dark?**

Fear is a normal response to a threatening situation. It is one of the basic human emotions. Talking about or playing out fears without condemnation or making fun of them help children alleviate and grow out of their fears.

Daydreaming

"We have had dreams, and there is no one to interpret them." And Joseph said to them, "Do not interpretations belong to God? Please tell them to me." (Gen. 40:8)

> Last night I had the strangest dream,
> My chairs and tables were ice cream,
> My bed was made of lollipops,
> And all my blocks were candy drops.
> The kitchen plates were apple pies,
> And every cup a root beer shake.
> My shoes were laced with licorice,
> My puppy was a chocolate cake.
> The wonder of a dream is this . . .
> That what we wish for IS!

Questions to Ponder: **What are your daydreams? your night dreams? your wishes that happen in your imagination?**

Every child enjoys daydreaming. Every child has a right to time and a place for daydreaming, for we can grant in fantasy what we cannot give in reality. A fed fantasy is essential to a person's whole development, for fantasy is the beginning of transformation. Children fulfill many of their needs through fantasy that helps them cope with the "no's" and "don'ts," the frustrations and failures from being small and unskilled. Children gratify their desires through daydreaming.

Fantasy helps fill huge gaps in the child's understanding that are due to inner pressures, immaturity, and lack of information. The child becomes comfortable with himself by spinning out daydreams and fantasizing, thus developing his inner resources, so that the emotions, intellect, and imagination support and enrich one another.

Every person needs a garden, a corner, a place in the mind set aside to dream and imagine. An exercised imagination produces faith and reveals deeper aspects of spiritual reality. It is the fundamental capacity for insight that is the source of all knowledge and love and meaning.

Each His Size

Everyone skips and jumps and runs and tries,
Everyone feels and dreams to just their size.

She was different from the rest of the children. She could not climb. She could not count. She did not speak. She was different from all of the other children, but she could smile. And her smile was different from all of the other children, for in her smile was her speech, her movement, and her thought.

She was different from all of the other children except in one thing, that which mattered most. She was loved!

Her parents loved her. Her teacher loved her. God loved her, and sometimes it seemed to those of us around her that perhaps God loved her a bit more than all the rest of us because she was . . . different.

Questions to Ponder: In what way are you different? Is it good to be different? Why?

THE WONDER OF DIFFERENCES
All around the wide world,
Far across the sea,
Children stop and wonder,
Questioning like me.
God, in all your wisdom,
Love, and power, and might,
Why did you create us
Brown, or black, or white?

P.S. I just saw a rainbow, God,
Shining over me.
If there were no differences,
A rainbow wouldn't be.

Every child is unique. Part of our task is to help children discover and develop their uniqueness.

"I'm me," said the child, "because I'm the only one who can say what I think."

I'm Glad

*I praise you, for I am fearfully
and wonderfully made. (Ps. 139:14a)*

The small, brown bunny was sad. He thought, "Brown is such a dull color!" especially when he saw the orange squirrel.

"Oh, if I had orange fur, then I would be happy!"

"Yes," said the orange squirrel. "I like my orange color," as he scampered up the tree to hide a nut.

The brown bunny watched the squirrel climb the tree and when he looked up, he saw a blue-feathered bird. "Oh, if I had blue fur, then I would be happy!"

"Yes," said the blue-feathered bird. "I like my blue color," as he flew to the pond for a drink of cool water.

The brown bunny followed the bird, hopping down the hill to the pond where he saw a green-backed turtle. "Oh, if I had green fur, then I would be happy!"

"Yes," said the green-backed turtle. "I like my green color," as she climbed upon a lily pad and floated across the pond.

Just then there was a shot! It was the hunters. They were looking for small, brown bunnies. It was too late to move, so the brown bunny stood perfectly still. And the hunters went past without even seeing the brown bunny!

"Be glad for your color brown that matches the ground just as I match the leaves in the fall," said the orange squirrel.

"Be glad for your color brown that matches the ground just as I match the sky through which I fly," said the blue-feathered bird.

"Be glad for your color brown that matches the ground just as I match the lily pad on which I lie."

"I am," said the small, brown bunny. "I am glad God planned me just the way I am!"[1]

(For added enjoyment make a brown bunny, orange squirrel, blue bird, green turtle, orange leaf, blue sky, and green lily pad from flannel for telling the story on a flannelboard.)

Questions to Ponder: What makes you glad? How are you special? Have you ever wanted to be different? How did the story end?

Pray: "Thank you, God, for our bodies and our minds, our souls and our strengths. Amen."

Real self-esteem is accepting oneself, being who one really is, without competing with others.

The life of feeling is the dominant way of knowing for children. It is the source of images that inform their world. Our primary task is to nourish the feeling, imaging powers of the individual with wonder and gratitude to God, which can lead the learner to an awareness of his or her own inner being and worth as a child of God.

Show It!

Happy are the people whose God is the LORD. (Ps. 144:15b)

Why are you so sad?" Mary asked Oscar at the fair.

Oscar was a clown. He had a large, painted, red mouth that fell at each side. Painted tears rolled down his cheeks from his crying eyes. Oscar looked so sad as he replied, "Inside I am happy."

"Show me!" said Mary.

Oscar clapped his two large, yellow, gloved hands together, but his mouth fell at the sides and his eyes had tears rolling down his cheeks.

"Here!" said Mary, looking at Oscar and suddenly feeling sad, as she handed Oscar her pink cotton candy.

"But inside I am happy," Oscar said, as Mary slowly and sadly walked away, feeling like an empty balloon. Mary had never been to a fair before. She did not know that clowns wore painted faces.

As her father lifted her onto the white horse on the merry-go-round, she heard her favorite song, "Mary Had a Little Lamb." The merry tune made her smile again, as she sang the happy words.

But when Mary got off the merry-go-round and could no longer hear the music, she thought about Oscar, and then she saw him talking with the elephant.

"Why are you so sad?" Mary asked again.

"My spirit inside is happy," Oscar replied, tears rolling down from his eyes.

"Show me!" she said.

Oscar jumped up and down, stomping his feet, but his mouth fell down at the sides and the tears rolled down from his eyes.

Mary shoved the stuffed brown bear her father had won for her into Oscar's arms and ran away quickly, feeling again like an empty balloon.

"Would you like to ride the elephant?" her father asked, seeing what had happened.

Mary agreed. Riding high above the people on the huge elephant made Mary happy and she laughed aloud.

But it was Oscar who helped Mary down from the elephant's back.

"Why are you so sad?" Mary asked again. Seeing the tears rolling down Oscar's cheeks, Mary began to cry.

"I am happy!" Oscar declared, but seeing Mary cry, suddenly Oscar felt sad inside.

Oscar reached into his large baggy pockets and took out a jar of white cream and a shiny mirror. "Please hold this for me," he said to Mary.

While Mary held the mirror, Oscar covered his face with the white cream and wiped away the painted tears rolling down his cheeks and the large red lips covering his mouth.

Mary looked at Oscar and laughed, as she began to sing, "If you're happy and you know it, then your face will surely show it. If you're happy and you know it, clap your hands."

Together Mary and Oscar clapped their hands, stomped their feet, and smiled at each other, feeling like full balloons.

Questions to Ponder: What does this story say to you? What makes you sad? Show it! What makes you happy? Show it! What made Mary cry? What made Oscar cry? How do you feel when you see people who are sad? What could we do when we see sadness?

Show an uninflated balloon. What does this balloon make you think or feel?

Blow it up. Now what do you think or feel?

Oscar said his "spirit" inside was happy. God blew breath into the first person and they became alive with God's spirit. When we care about sadness, we are showing God's spirit of love that is inside of us.

Children will not understand but intuit what we are saying, as we introduce them to a religious vocabulary. Language, our questions and our answers, halts behind intuition and feelings. Yet expressions of intuition require language, so we use metaphors and symbols to speak and write of that which is beyond speech and language, beyond explanation.

Religion is a process, the process of living life with reverence. It grows daily without our awareness, as Jesus said, "So is the kingdom of God as if a man should sleep and rise night and day, and the seed should sprout and grow up, he knows not how" (based on Mark 4:26).

Self-Image

"As the Father has loved me, so I have loved you." (John 15:9)

*T*he restaurant was crowded with grown-ups. As the child walked to the table all he could see were legs. He stretched his small body from the seat to reach the spoon. His parents were engaged in conversation and he felt very small. When the waitress came to the table, she smiled at the boy and asked, "May I take your order, sir?"

The child looked at his mother. His mother was talking.

"What would you like to order?" the waitress asked again.

A wide smile spread across his face and he pulled at his mother's arm. The diners stopped their conversation when they heard the young boy shout at his parents, "Look Mommy and Daddy, I'm real! I'm real!"

Questions to Ponder: Have you ever felt like the child in the story? What makes you feel "real"? What do you like to do best?

Children who know the presence and love of God from their earliest days are never alone. Because of God's love and their vivid imaginations, they accept the things they cannot see.

Children's self-esteem is based on their self-image.

It isn't enough for children to be loved. They must feel loved, feel that they matter and are competent. Children need unconditional love in place of earned love. Self-esteem is not built on love that is based on their behavior. "I love you if . . . " or "I love you when . . . "

The child was to write five spelling words five times. She had finished three of the words when her teacher said, "Susan, you have two to go."

Susan looked up at her teacher and said, "Teacher, why do you notice what I haven't done, rather than what I do?"

The child knew the importance of affirmation. Children create and learn in their own ways by trying out and trying on. Negative criticism blocks creativity.

Brad was four and Hal was seven. They lived in a family with high expectations. Hal met these expectations and excelled, but Brad felt that he could not do as well as was expected of him and retreated from the attempt to do so.

Crumpling the painting he had just finished in nursery school, Brad threw it into the wastebasket. Because Brad was not satisfied with himself, he was dissatisfied with his work. The fact that Brad did as well as the other children and as well as his brother at that age was secondary

67

to his feelings. Because of his feelings of failure, he failed. Because Brad felt unaccepted as he was, his behavior became unacceptable.

The way children think grows from the quality of their firsthand experiences, for the child is a total person. How the child feels about himself affects his success or failure in the experience. Any "I can do it!" experience is an important factor in the child's growth development. The sense of self-esteem, of positive self-worth, is the foundation for all subsequent learning.

The Hill

"For I know the plans I have for you, says the LORD, *plans for welfare and not for evil, to give you a future and a hope." (Jer. 29:11 RSV)*

It is too high! I cannot climb the hill. I can't do it!" the boy insisted, looking up at the high hill.

"Don't worry," his sister assured him. "Let's play a game instead. See how I leave my footprint in the sand."

The boy who was also barefoot made his print in the sand.

"Look, my print is deeper," she cried, taking another step.

"You are heavier," said the boy, trying again.

"Look here!" they continued to cry at one another, matching footprints, until the boy, looking around in surprise, said, "We're at the top of the hill. We did it!"

"Dear me, so we did," said his sister.

Questions to Ponder: What is the hardest thing for you to do? Why? Have you ever said, "I can't" and then tried and did. How did you feel? What made you succeed? Do you think God wants us to keep trying?

Hope keeps one going, one step at a time. Stories provide hope. The format of the fairy tale is three tries. It says you may not win the first time, nor the second, but persist, be patient, postpone gratification, hope, and try again.

Hope is a powerful creative force, for it provides the energy and purpose for us to plan. It gives a sense of possibility and enlarges our capacity to receive. Once, when I was exhausted and discouraged, I dreamed I was drowning. I cried for help and for someone to throw me a life jacket. Instead I heard Jesus say, "I taught you how to swim and I am with you."

Jesus came to Peter when he was sinking in the water and crying for help, and Jesus will come to you and me. As Jesus pulled Peter to safety, Jesus pulls us toward wholeness and healing.

Hope is the heart and center of the human being. The nature of hope is to imagine what has not yet come to pass but still is possible, a future good realistically possible but not yet visible.

So we tell our stories that help us connect with one another. Some heal, some affirm, some teach, as we do in their telling. In our wandering and wondering, we need the hearing and the telling to remind us that we are not alone in our search for meaning, identity, and hope on "the way" to our final destination.

To Clap and Cheer

For you shall go out in joy, . . . and all the trees of the field shall clap their hands. (Isa. 55:12)

Her dream was to be in the school play. Her heart was in her dream. Her mother feared for her chances of being chosen but said nothing.

On the day the parts were assigned her mother was ready and waiting for her daughter at the door.

Emily's eyes were shining with pride and excitement. As she hugged her mother, she exclaimed, "I've been chosen to clap and cheer!"

Questions to Ponder: How did that story make you feel? Share some of your times of clapping and cheering. What questions would you like to ask?

To clap is an important activity in the church, at school, at home, wherever we are. The psalmists did it when they praised God.

In one church school class the children clap when everyone is present. If one is missing, there is no clapping, for the class is diminished. I think this group experienced, and thus, understood the story of the good shepherd and the one lost lamb.

Self-esteem is also rooted in omnipotent fantasy: "I can do anything!" At the count of "One, two, three, let go . . . " my baby grandson Tiuh stood alone, his face a rapture of pure joy, as if to say, "I am the greatest!" His grandmother agreed.

69

The most important factor in the growth of a healthy child is a positive sense of self, high self-worth and confidence. "I like me."

Two children came to school and met their teacher for the first time. One saw a stranger. The other saw a friend. How one perceives life and reality is based on one's self-confidence. In a sense there are two kinds of persons: those who see strangers and are afraid and those who see friends and affirm.

Self-esteem is rooted in good object relations. When there is someone in the child's world who is a reliable source of love, self-esteem is developed.

Accept children as they are. Look for their strong points. Notice what they can do, such as "clap and cheer," rather than what they cannot do. This is modeling what we teach.

Truth

Jesus said . . . , "I am the way, and the truth, and the life." (John 14:6)

*O*nce there was a shepherd boy. He took care of the sheep. He led them to water so they could drink and to grass they could eat. He had a crook, which is a cane with a question mark top that he used to pull the sheep out of the bushes when they were caught.

One day when nothing was happening and he was bored, he had an idea. He called in a loud voice, "A lion! A lion is stealing one of my sheep."

The people who were working in the fields heard him and they came running to help him.

"I tricked you! I tricked you! There is no lion."

The people had left their work to help him and they were upset that he had pulled this trick on them. They returned to their work and the shepherd returned to taking care of his sheep.

So the days passed. "There's nothing to do," the young shepherd complained to the wind. Then he smiled, remembering how he had tricked the people.

"The lion! The lion is eating my sheep!" he cried in a loud voice.

The people, working in the fields, heard the shepherd and left their work to come to help him.

"I tricked you! I tricked you! There is no lion."

The people looked at one another. They did not like being tricked. In an angry mood they returned to their work.

So the days passed. "I am a clever lad," thought the boy. "I tricked the people!"

The shepherd boy recalled the people running to help him. "There are no lions . . . around . . . here," he thought, as he saw something, something very large, creeping toward one of his sheep. "It couldn't be . . . it looks like a lion, but . . . "

Then he saw . . . it was a lion!

The shepherd boy cried as loud as he could, "A lion! A lion is eating my sheep!"

The people heard. The people smiled at one another and nodded their heads. Of course, another trick!

This time no one ran to help the shepherd. This time the lion ate the lamb. This time the owner of the sheep was very angry at the shepherd boy. From that day on, the shepherd learned to tell the truth.

Questions to Ponder: What did you hear in that story? What is the importance of telling the truth?

As I ended the story of the shepherd boy and the lion "at the altar" in the church worship service, Rebecca stood up to leave. She suddenly turned to me and asked, "Was it true?"

I replied, "It may not be factual, Rebecca, but it is true."

Telling the truth is a long process of learning, but yet I think children, such as Rebecca, are more honest than adults.

Waiting

Our soul waits for the LORD; he is our help and shield. (Ps. 33:20)

> Why, when I want, must I always wait?
> The summer waits for the spring to end,
> The winter waits for the fall,
> The flowers wait for the sun and rain,
> The small bird waits for the call
> Of his mate.
> All things wait;
> And I wait for thee, O Lord.

No more waiting!" wailed Will. Will was weary of waiting. "I have to wait for dinner. I have to wait until I grow up. I have to wait for my birthday and Christmas and summer and all I seem to do is wait!" Even his name was . . . William Warren Wate!

So William decided to move down the street to the Hurry house. He knocked on the door and it opened in a hurry. "Well, Will, what do you want? Speak up. Hurry!"

Will quickly told Mrs. Hurry what he wanted and she told him to come inside quickly and shut the door. Now William no longer had to wait. He did not have to wait to grow up in order to stay up late, for he could stay up as late as he liked. But he was always tired and grouchy the next day and he hated to hurry getting up.

William did not have to wait his turn on the swing. Chuck, Buck, and Harry Hurry all sat on the swing with William at the same time. But William fell off and skinned his arm and knee, and there was no time to take care of the hurt because of the hurry.

William did not have to wait for dinner. The Hurrys ate all day long, but William went to bed with a stomachache.

William did not have to wait for his birthday. The Hurrys sang "Happy Birthday, dear William" every day and his birthday no longer seemed special.

William did not have to wait for Christmas. The Hurrys kept their tree up all year long and sang Christmas carols every day, so that Christmas no longer seemed special. There was no one to take time to tell stories or take long, looking walks, and no one to take the time to talk with or listen to William's prayers. It was just "Hurry, hurry, hurry!" So William slowly packed his suitcase and returned to the Wate house.

He slowly walked down the street, and slowly knocked on the door.

"William!" his mother exclaimed. "How good to see you," she said, as she hugged him.

"William!" said his father, putting down his newspaper. "Now I can tell stories tonight."

"William!" cried his brother. "If you can wait until I find my shoes, we can take a long, looking walk."

William said, "I'll wait. There are two things you can't hurry. You can't hurry growing up and, as the song says, you can't hurry love!"

Questions to Ponder: What is the hardest thing for you to wait for? What did William learn? Would you like to move to the Hurry house? Do you live in the Wate house or the Hurry house? Why do we have to wait? What do you do when you have to wait? For what are you waiting now?

The children waited with great excitement for the baby chicks to hatch. When the process seemed to be at last underway, two of the children, in their impatience, decided to help the hatching along by peeling the shell after the first cracks appeared. When the teacher discovered what had happened, it was too late. Two of the seven chicks died. The teacher said to a parent present, "It takes time to grow so we do well to remember the inner wisdom of nature and respect the natural rhythm of growing."

Waiting with trust in God is nurtured by prayer and sustained by the life of the imagination. We grow from the inside out. Growth is part of God's plan for life. When children learn trust, growing from inside out, they develop in their own unique ways.

Waiting, the ability to tolerate postponement or failure, is an absolute essential in all growth. Hurry prevents appreciation of today, in the possibilities of living life abundantly.

The first year I taught kindergarten in a church setting I opened our morning with daily "hurried" prayer, fearful of disruption from restless five-year-olds. Several weeks passed before Debbie at last said, "Teacher, you always say *Amen* just as I get started thinking."

God gives us many gifts, and the gift of patience is a precious gift, the wisdom of waiting a priceless wonder.

We Are Special

When I look at your heavens, the work of your fingers,
the moon and the stars that you have established;
what are human beings that you . . . care for them? . . .
and crowned them with glory and honor. (Ps. 8:3-5)

> Mother says, "It will all even out."
> Grandma says, "Looks are only skin deep."
> Dad says, "You are beautiful."
> But these are only words.
> When I look in the mirror,
> The words disappear, and all I see is me.
> God, why did you make some people pretty
> And some smart and some creative?
> And then there is me.
> Mom says, "It is heredity" and wishes she
> Were prettier so I would be.
> But, God, my mom is beautiful inside.
> Maybe that's the best "heredity."

Freckles

*H*er face was covered with warm, brown spots called "freckles."

Over and over friends and strangers would say, "Hi, Freckles," not knowing the hurt caused by feeling she was different.

"Look, your spots are growing," Carrie laughed one day, as Amy and she were playing.

Amy had been running. Her cheeks were red and the funny little freckles on her nose did seem to be getting bigger. Amy ran home in tears. "I'm not funny looking, am I?" Amy cried at her mother.

The freckles disappeared beneath the tears. Mother looked at the tears and remembered the tears that she had shed for the same reason. Mother, too, had freckles. She wanted to wrap her daughter in her arms and cry together. Instead she remembered her mother's words. "Am I funny looking?" she asked.

"No, you're beautiful, but Carrie laughed at my freckles."

Mother knew that she was not beautiful except in Amy's eyes, but she knew, too, that there were many different kinds of beauty. "Your freckles make friends happy. They are so sunny and friendly, they make people feel glad."

"And laugh?"

"Laughing is a way to bring the inside happiness out. We feel good when we laugh. You can feel good that you help your friends feel good, thanks to your freckles."

Amy looked into the mirror at her funny freckles. "I'm lucky I have freckles," she exclaimed, smiling. "Freckles are a sign of friendship."

Questions to Ponder: What did Amy's freckles mean to her when she cried? What is unique (different) about you? Has anyone ever laughed or made fun of you? What did you do?

Sometimes after hearing the poem the children will respond with, "I feel that way. I would like to be pretty (or smart, or a fast runner, and so on)." The adult is tempted to refute the statement or compliment the speaker, but instead ask, "Does anyone else feel as if they lack something they would like?"

Other children may respond and children can be helped to see that they are not alone in their feelings. Knowing that others lack and wish for things can help children face the fact that it is all right to wish and dream. Some of the children may even comment, "I think you are pretty (or smart, or whatever)." A compliment from one's peer group is more readily accepted than from an adult who "always says that."

Children are curious about themselves, for their self-esteem is built on the impressions they receive from others. Amy was building positive self-esteem, which is built on the picture children discover and create through the actions and words of persons they encounter.

The child had bright red hair and a stranger, stooping down to speak to the child, asked, "Where did you get your beautiful hair?" to which the child replied, "It came with my face."

You Can Do It!

> *Know that the LORD is God.*
> *It is he that made us, and we are his. (Ps. 100:3a)*

I can't do it!" he cried.

Brad was learning to ride a bicycle with his mother's help. As long as she held onto the bike, he was fine. When she let go, he did too.

The bumps he took hurt his body, but his sense of failure hurt even more.

His mother thought and then she prayed silently, "God help me and help Brad."

"Try again," she suggested aloud.

"I can't do it!" he insisted, refusing to try again, because it hurt.

Over and over she helped him, but at last she said to him, "Do you really believe that God chose you from all the boys and girls in the world to be the one who couldn't ride a bike?"

Then the mother went inside and Brad rode away on his bicycle.

Questions to Ponder: Have you ever said or felt, "I can't do it!" I felt that way when I was learning to tie my shoes. I felt I was a complete failure. What did the mother do to help Brad? How have you been helped to keep trying until you can?

Trusting God's love can help us defeat fear. God empowers us to think for ourselves, ask help from others when we need it, and let go what is not in our power to do at the time. God works through us to build the future. God helps us hope, and as we believe our hope into existence, we help to create its reality.

Believing they can, children are encouraged to try: I had been away from home for three weeks and the suitcase was so heavy I could hardly carry it, for halfway through the trip I had jammed as much as I could from two suitcases into one and sent the other case home. As I walked,

75

the bag became heavier and heavier and I switched it from hand to hand, finally carrying it in my arms as if a chunk of marble.

When I arrived home it was good to see my six-year-old neighbor, Sarah.

"I'll carry it, Elaine!" she shouted, picking up my suitcase, as she has always insisted upon doing since she was three, for Sarah is a determined child.

"No, Sarah, it is too heavy!" I protested, reaching for the suitcase.

The small child picked up the suitcase and walked to the door. I stood there in amazement.

Sarah has always believed "I can do it!" and that belief gives her the strength and the courage to try, and most of the time, to succeed.

When Sarah was learning to dive at age five, her friend Tova remarked, "I wish I could dive as well as you."

Sarah replied, "You can. Just say 'Tova, you can do it!' That's what I say. 'Sarah, you can do it!' "

Embracing the Church

In the church of Jesus Christ children find love, a sense of belonging, stewardship, wonder, the word and presence of God, music, prayer, and Jesus' message and mission.

Do you believe in God?" the teacher asked.
The child replied, "Yes!"
"Why do you believe in God?" the teacher asked.
The child thought a moment and then said, "I don't know why. I think it runs in the family."

Religion that "runs in the family" encourages children to develop the inner resources they need to face the crises and traumas of life.

Children and adults do not grow in a vacuum. We make intelligent decisions through the opportunity of choice, but we cannot choose wisely what we have not experienced.

Poems and parables about the church can help children experience their sense of not only being at church but of being the church.

Church

O LORD, I love the house in which you dwell. (Ps. 26:8)

> I'm thinking of a friendly place
> That's made of brick or stone,
> Of people who have come to share,
> A room where I am known.
> It's where we talk about the things
> That I see every day,

77

And often I have thought about,
Without the words to say.
It's where they like me as I am,
Accepting what I do.
It's where I feel God's love and care,
And learn to love God, too.
It's where we praise and sing and pray
Beneath the chapel dome.
O Lord, I love your dwelling place,
The church . . . the world . . . your home!

Questions to Ponder: Why do *you* go to church?

*W*here's him going?" *two-year-old William asked his mother, as his father started off to church.*

"To church," his mother replied.

"Whuz him going to get there?" William wanted to know. At the store we get food, at the library we get books, at the gas station, gas. What do we get at church?

At church we get questions and answers and assurances of trust in God.

"My mother made me go to Sunday school and church. Believe me, I am not going to force my children. They can make up their own minds!" the father declared, yawning, turning over in bed, and returning to sleep that Sunday morning.

But at breakfast when Amy picked at her eggs, Father said sternly, "Eat your eggs, Amy. They are good for you!"

Father would decide for Amy the physical food she would receive to support her body until the next meal, but Amy could decide whether or not she would receive spiritual food to support her through failure and loss and loneliness, through struggling to find meaning in her life, and through suffering.

Children need the strength and source of comfort that only worshiping God can give.

The family had not attended church for several years. As they walked toward the church door, William opened it, looked up at his father, and asked, "Do you think God still remembers me?"

Religion is not a series of answers to questions. It is the experience of wonder and gratitude, pain and sorrow, joy and love, mourned and celebrated within the family of faith.

The Sacrament of Holy Communion

While they were eating, he took a loaf of bread, and after blessing it he broke it, gave it to them, and said, "Take; this is my body." Then he took a cup, and after giving thanks he gave it to them, and all of them drank from it. He said to them, "This is my blood of the covenant, which is poured out for many [all]. Truly I tell you, I will never again drink of the fruit of the vine until that day when I drink it new in the kingdom of God." (Mark 14:22-25).

As you read the scripture story have a loaf of bread. When Jesus breaks the bread for his friends in the story, hold the bread and break the loaf in half. At the end break off a piece for each child, saying, "This is a symbol for the body of Christ. Take. Eat."

God invites all to share "bread" at the Banquet of Life. Jesus taught his friends and us to pray, "Give us this day our daily bread." He ate with his friends, for eating together was important. Jesus' ancestors believed that when two or three ate together, God was present. The Hebrews believed that when a host or hostess invited someone to eat, they were saying to that person, "You are my sister, my brother. I will take care of you." He invites us to eat of his "body" in Holy Communion, for "all things are ready."

The four-year-old knelt beside her grandmother at the communion railing. When the pastor passed by her without offering her bread or drink, she turned to her grandmother and in a loud, puzzled whisper said, "But Mumsie, I didn't get nothing again."

Worship is to gather the people of God,
   break the bread of the sacrament of Jesus the Christ,
    and tell the story of God's love and Spirit among and within us here and now.

***Questions to Ponder:* What is communion? What is worship? How do you worship? What is your favorite part of the worship service? What is your favorite object in the sanctuary? Why?**

Children think concretely. They see pictures in their minds. Though they do not understand the abstract words used, they see what is happening. People leave their seats to come to the communion table.

They see the congregation on their knees, praying, eating the bread and drinking from the cup.

Children are part of the family of God and as part of that family, they belong at the altar where the entire family has gathered to celebrate their Lord's coming in the bread, again and again. When children participate they also taste and join as members of the congregation of faith in the fellowship of belonging.

Confirmation

"Choose this day whom you will serve." (Josh. 24:15)

> Today you've taken a special step,
> You've made a special vow,
> You've said to God, before us all,
> "I'm part of your church now."
> And though it's never ended,
> This learning how
> To be God's own,
> You've taken one large, giant leap toward God
> Together, and alone.

Did you really say that, Dad?" Brad wanted to know. He was very excited, because Brad and his brother, Andy, wanted to go to the football game. "Stop teasing me, Andy. You know I want to see that game and Dad said he was too busy."

"It's true. Dad said so," Andy repeated.

*"Did you really say that, Dad?" he asked again. Brad wanted **confirmation**. He wanted to hear Dad say the words for himself.*

Dad laughed. "Yes, I did say that. I promised we would go to the game. But why didn't you believe Andy?" his father asked.

"I wanted to hear it from you in order to be sure. I wanted you to confirm what Andy had said for you!"

Questions to Ponder: **Con-fir-ma-tion is an act in which a person "confirms" for himself or herself the vows of church membership that were said for the individual when he or she was baptized. What does the word confirm mean to you?**

80

The church, God's people, want to make sure that those who join as members of the Body of Christ know what they are joining, what is required of them if they join, and why it is important for them to join the church. The rite of confirmation is a matter of the heart, an acknowledgment in public of one's personal relationship with God: Creator, Redeemer, and Spirit.

It is a matter of the mind, as well, a commitment to what the church believes and does, and a matter of the will; a living, active awareness of and participation in the work of God in the world. It is saying "Yes!" to God.

> Jesus lived so you could know God's love,
> Live in God's kindgom now.
> What will you do?
> Will you say "yes" or "no"?
> Accept God's grace?
> Enter God's kingdom now and seek to grow
> In love and faithfulness?
> To work and change the world toward God?
> Then say your "YES!" with us.

God is always saying "yes" to us, confirming who we are and what we do. When you say "yes," you take the responsibility for being a child of God for yourself, loving and trusting God, serving God by loving and serving your neighbor. It means celebrating life by saying "yes" to God's good gifts and thanking God for them with your whole life.

If Coins Could Talk

Nevertheless he regarded their distress
when he heard their cry. (Ps. 106:44)

Use flannel figures or pictures backed with flannel to place on a flannelboard as you say the words to the fingerplay: a church, Bible, globe, pastor, and songbook, as well as a hand holding coins:

> The coins we brought to church today,
> If they could talk, what would they say?
> This one might say, "I heat the church or keep it cool."
> This one might say, "I buy the Bibles for our school."

> This one might say, "I go around the world to share
> the good news of God's loving care."
> This one might say, "I pay the minister to preach,
> marry, bury, baptize, teach."
> This one might say, "I buy the books we use to sing and pray."
> If coins could talk, perhaps that's what they'd say.[1]

Once upon a time there was a village and in this village some of the people had food, good food—milk, apples, bananas, and pizza—and some of the people had little to eat and were very hungry.

In that same village some of the children went to school so they could learn to read and write, and some of the children searched through the garbage on street corners or worked in dark, dingy, dirty places.

In this village some of the people wore warm clothing and listened to lovely music, while in the same village some of the people had nothing to wear and heard only cruel, ugly words and cries of pain.

The people who wore fine clothing and ate good food and attended beautiful schools lived in lovely homes. The people who had no food or clothes or schools to attend, lived in crowded places or had no homes at all.

One day a father and his child came to visit the village. They saw the rich people and they saw the poor people, and as they were leaving the village, the child asked the father, "Why are some of the people rich and some of the people poor?"

The father did not know and he shook his head to say so.

"Why don't the rich people who have warm and friendly homes and schools help the poor who have none?" the child asked the father.

The father looked back at the village called "Earth" and shook his head again. He was silent for he had no answer.

Questions to Ponder: Do you have an answer for the father and the child? Ask the children to say the words "If Coins Could Talk" with you as you repeat the poem above. Why do we bring our coins to church? What do our coins do?

Sometimes the church is called the "body" or "hands" of Christ in the world. To be part of the church is to affirm what the church affirms, to confirm your "adoption" by God at baptism into the "body" of Christ at work in the world today.

If I Were the Church

For as in one body we have many members, and not all the members have the same function, so we, who are many, are one body in Christ, and individually we are members one of another. (Rom. 12:4-5)

If I were the church,
My church bells would ring,
"Come everyone," I'd gladly sing.
(Place hands together and swing arms.)

If I were the church,
I'd stretch my arms wide (Stretch arms to sides.)
To welcome everyone inside.

If I were the church,
But I am, you see,
For the church is people, you and you
And you and me. (Point to others and self.)[2]

Questions to Ponder: What is the church?

Listen to the following poem and see what it says to you:

Home is where we like to be
In rain and stormy weather,
Feeling safe and comfortable
Whenever we're together.
Home is where the family,
The father and the mother,
Show and teach their children to
Love and help each other.
And church too is a home
Where families are living
In the way that Jesus taught,
Loving and forgiving.
What is the church? (building, people, a family)

One day a child asked his father, "Why do I have to go to church?" and his father replied, "I would rather fly with a pilot who has had lessons than with one who has not. I would rather learn about the Christian faith from a fellow Christian than from 'the one in the street.' "

Mother added, "Going to church is something our family does together."

So the child went to church. He supported the church with his presence, his gifts, and his service.

And one day he answered his own child who asked, "Why do we go to church?"

The Sacrament of Baptism

Then Jesus came from Galilee to John at the Jordan, to be baptized by him. (Matt. 3:13)

*I*t is he!"

The man in the river climbed out of the water. He shook the water from his long, wet hair and his long beard and from the camel's hair that covered his body. "What are you doing here?" he cried in amazement.

"I have come to be baptized," the man replied.

"I cannot baptize you," exclaimed John, who was called "the Baptist."

The man smiled at John. He was not upset by John's words. "Now is the time, John. The time is at hand."

"I need to be baptized by you and you come to me?" John asked.

"It is according to God's plan," the man replied.

John did as the man said. He took his hand and led him into the water. "I baptize you in the name of God." John stopped suddenly. The people were looking up. A small white dove flew out of the clouds. It flew down to the man's shoulder.

The people began to whisper, "I heard a voice!"

"So did I," others whispered.

"What did you hear?"

"I thought that I heard, 'This is my son. I am well pleased.' "

The people grew silent as John the Baptist began to speak. "Jesus of Nazareth, I baptize you in God's name. Amen."

> Into the water stepped the man
> To be baptized into God's plan.
> Out of the heavens came the dove,
> As Jesus heard with joy and love,
> "This is my chosen, beloved one,
> Who pleases me. This is my son!"[3]

***Questions to Ponder:* What is the meaning of "baptism"? Are there any questions you would like to ask?**

Provide paper and crayons for children to draw a "welcoming" picture for the one baptized. Give it to the child's parents (or child) at the end of the service.

Through baptism we receive a new identity. When a baby is born, a bracelet with the baby's family name is placed on its wrist in order to identify the baby. We know to whose family the baby belongs. When a person is baptized, water is placed on the person in order to give him or her a new identity. We know to whom this person belongs. Baptism means we have joined a very large family that extends around the world. Having been loved, we respond with love out of gratitude, and even that is God's grace, for God is Creator and Lord of all—the ordinary and the extraordinary, who loves us with unconditional love.

Tell stories about baptisms in which you have participated.

Children learn by their senses and by participation. To fully participate in the act of baptism invite children to sit at the front of the congregation or to come up around the baptismal font during the baptism in order to feel the importance of this sacrament and become involved in its symbolism.

Baptism is the church's sacrament of response to God's love. Through water, the symbol of new life, and words, the baptized one is blessed by the Spirit into a new perspective of life and the world.

God's grace frees us to let go of our selfish needs and desires to care for others, and to take the risk of loving.

Together

Now you are the body of Christ and individually members of it. (1 Cor. 12:27)

There once was a man who loved God. Because he loved God, he loved other people, too.

One day he met a sick man. "I will help you," he said, because he loved God. But the sick man needed medicine and a doctor and a place where he could get well.

The man said, "I will build a hospital. But I cannot build a hospital alone. I need others who will help me."

The man found other people who loved God. Because they loved God, they loved others, too.

Together they built a hospital. Together they bought medicine. Together they paid the doctors and the nurses who cared for the sick.

There were many things the man could do alone to show his love. There were many things he needed others to help him do.

The church is like that. The church is people who love God and serve and help others alone and together.

Questions to Ponder: **What is the task (job) of the church? How can you and I help?**

The church is the "hug" of God incarnated and lived out in its people. Where there is no lap or hug, the church has failed. The church's mission is to be the embodiment of God's grace, as the sacraments are.

When Jesus described discipleship, he hugged a child, saying, "Whoever welcomes in my name one of these children, welcomes me" (Mark 9:37 GNB). Children belong to the worship community. They worship by belonging. Children feel a sense of belonging when they are included through smiles, handshakes, Holy Communion, and stories.

Children experience, feel, and then learn. Worship cannot be "taught" in a vacuum. We learn to worship by worshiping, and the ability to feel love and wonder, the basis of worship, precedes a rational understanding of worship. The nature of the church and the good news of Scripture are both based on faith in God's unconditional love and acceptance of all people. Children need and deserve the strength and source of comfort that only trust in God can give, for the church is the "lap" of God.

Words

God said to Moses, "I AM WHO I AM." (Exod. 3:14a)

*E*very Sunday at church the woman told her grandson, "Be good. This is God's house."

That afternoon, as he rode past the church, the boy became very excited. It was not surprising, for he had seen God!

"There's God!" he shouted, pointing toward the church.

The mother quickly put on the brakes to stop the car. "Where?" she asked with intense interest.

"There!" he cried again, pointing to the church. "There! God is mowing the lawn."

The boy had seen his father mowing the lawn at home. Here was a man mowing the lawn at God's house, therefore, the man must be God.

Perhaps he was right, in part, or perhaps we should use words we all understand.

Questions to Ponder: **Can you see God? Can anyone see God? How do you know God?**

Because religious terms are abstract and metaphorical, children are confused. Children think concretely, in pictures, in images. They learn through what they can see and touch, and understanding God is the work of a lifetime. Relationship with God is life's most essential work.

The church speaks and teaches metaphors that open the way to discovering what reality and vision the words evoke and reveal. Using metaphor, there are many names we give to God: Holy One, Creator, King, Friend, Lord, the Ground of Being, and most often "Help!" God as Father is a term of personal relationship, guiding, comforting, correcting, and challenging. Sometimes we use the term "Parent" or "Mother" for that relationship, as well.

Our ancient ancestors of the faith, living in mountainous Palestine, called God "the Rock of salvation." In the Old Testament God is known as Creator, Judge, Rock. In the New Testament God is the One who loves. In John's vision, the Revelation of Jesus Christ, the "throne" is used for the word "God." In other words, "the One who reigns." Jesus said, "God is love." The psalmist affirmed that God is the one who loves.

We attempt to explain God by what God does, so we say God is like a gardener. We see the flowers, even when we do not see the gardener. God is like an author. We read God's words, even when we do not see the author. God is like a poet, painter, creator, the wind, love, provider, but God is so great that we cannot define God. God is that and always more than that and different from that.

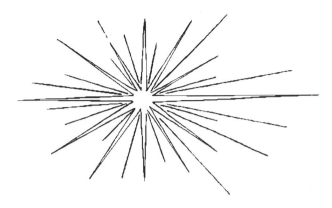

Encountering God

When my friend Sarah was twelve, she asked her mother if she had to believe in God, and her mother replied, "No, but it will be very lonely."

Stories help us encounter God and know that we are not alone. God is Creator. God said, "Let us make humankind in our image (Gen. 1:26)." The relationship with God, Creator, helps us discover our identity as creatures who create, as cocreators. Created in the "image of God" we are called upon to use our creativity, our imagination. Imagination and faith are deeply linked. Faith and imagination help us see another world in which we live, a world seen with the spirit and touched by the heart.

Judaism does not answer the question, "Who is God?" Instead it helps people to discover "How do we respond to God in our lives? How do we recognize God in our lives?"

Many children possess a special sense of the world, for children experience before they know and know before they conceptualize. The intellect may inform, but it is the imagination that comforts, for language halts behind imagination.

Much of our faith language is beyond the understanding of children. Through conversation they communicate their understandings. Conversation can be encouraged by asking appropriate questions, such as "What do you see?" or "What do you feel or think?"

When Jesus was questioned about his stories, he said, "He who has ears, let him hear." What matters is what the seer sees and the hearer hears.

Be with Me

Even though I walk through the darkest valley,
 I fear no evil;
for you are with me. (Ps. 23:4)

Dear God, when I hear funny noises in the night
And see strange shapes and shadows, black and white,
And wish with all my heart that it were light,
Be with me, God.
When I have dreams that frighten me,
And hear the thunder and see the lightning,
And wish for Mother and my family,
Be with me, God.
When I'm afraid and wonder what to do,
And think perhaps, others may be, too,
I close my eyes, remembering You
Are with me, God!

Questions to Ponder: When do you want God to be with you? God's promise is to be with us whenever we are afraid or love or look for help.

Poetry has the power to evoke in its hearers deep emotional responses. It is an invitation to talk together about the things we fear, the things we wish for, even the things we dislike and hate. In discussing the poem, some of the children said:
"I don't like the dark."
"I have bad dreams at night."
"I hate to be alone at night."
Poetry is a way of identifying our own thoughts and feelings. To know that others feel and think the way we do is consoling to children.
Children also like the rhyme, rhythm, and repetition of poems.
Nursery rhymes are the child's first introduction to the sounds and senses of poetry that one day will lead to a deep appreciation of the book of poems in our sacred Scriptures, the book of Psalms.
The poem "Be With Me" expresses what many of the psalms express, a longing for God.
Encourage the child to create his or her own prayer poem. When Hilda Conkling was six years old, she wrote this poem:

The world turns softly
Not to spill its lakes and rivers. The water is held in its arms

And the sky is held in the waters.
What is water,
That pours silver,
And can hold the sky?[1]

Colors

For everything there is a season, and a time for every matter under heaven.
(Eccles. 3:1)

a time for blue, and a time for green;
a plan for yellow, and a plan for red;
a time for black, and a time for pink;
a time for orange . . .

Before telling the story, give each of the participants a crayon or piece of construction paper in blue, green, black, red, yellow, orange, or pink. Ask the children to help you tell the story by holding up their color when they hear it named in the story:

All of the colors were happy: orange and red, green and yellow, black and pink. They sang and danced all day. They were happy because God said, "Orange, you will be the color of the peach and the pumpkin and the leaves in the fall." And orange was happy because God had a plan for orange.

"Green, you will be the color of growing things; the peas and the beans, the grass and the leaves." And green was happy because God had a plan for green.

"Yellow, you will be the color of the sun that causes all things to grow and warms the earth," God told the color yellow. And yellow was happy because God had a plan for yellow.

"Red, you will be the color of hot fire that heats the homes and cooks the food." And red was happy because God had a plan for red.

"Pink, you will be the color of the sunset in the evening and the sunrise in the morning," and pink was happy because God had a plan for pink.

"Black, you will be the color of the dark and quiet night when all things rest," and black was happy because God had a plan for black.

All of the colors were happy, pink and black, green and yellow, orange and red . . . all of the colors but blue. Blue was so sad he/she thought God had forgotten. But it was blue who forgot to trust the Creator, for God said, "Blue, I have saved you for last. You will be the color of the sea and the sky that covers all." And blue was happy because God had a plan for blue.

Now all of the colors were happy, for God had a plan for each of them, for you know, that's the way God is.[2]

Questions to Ponder: **What is your favorite color? How does it make you feel? Does God have a plan for you? Does God care about what you do?**

Sing: "Tell me why the fire is red
And grass and leaves are green instead.
Tell me why the sky's so blue?
And I will tell you why I love you."

Close your eyes and imagine a gray world. How does that make you feel? Why is fire red, leaves and grass green, and sky blue? Why did God create? Why do I love you?

A mother told how her three-year-old would look up at the sky from time to time and wave to God, calling, "Hey, Mom, God's looking at me."

The story "Colors" says that God is not only looking, but loving, and planning, because that is the way God is, a Maker.

"Creator" is one of the names we give God. Throughout the ages, myths, metaphors, and symbols have given us a way of thinking and talking about the unknown, a way of expressing a truth beyond the literal. In the Old Testament there is a rich diversity of images for God: thunder, lion, torrent, bear, ocean, king, judge, husband, master, shepherd, rock, fortress, lover, midwife, bird, door, wind, Creator, Almighty King, Love, a piling up in order to avoid idolatry and to express the complexity and richness of the divine-human relationship.

Metaphors are not descriptions but attempts to express the unfamiliar in terms of the familiar. Many images are necessary because all of them are partial, a way of speaking about the Great Unknown. They are never identity statements but ways of seeing something in terms of something else.

God Is Here

"The wind blows where it chooses, and you hear the sound of it, but you do not know where it comes from or where it goes." (John 3:8a)

*T*he child ate the cookies and milk that had been left on the table, as he played with his friend. When he returned home that afternoon, he told his mother about

the experience. "Johnny's mother wasn't there, but I know he has a mother."
"Why do you say that?" questioned his mother.
  "I knew she was there because she had left us food to eat."

Questions to Ponder: How do we know God is with us? What are some of the ways we know God's love and presence? Johnny's mother couldn't be seen, just as we do not "see" God, but the child knew that Johnny had a mother, as we know God is with us.

KNOWING
When the wind blows, leaves fly and bend,
Though I have never seen the wind.
When people love and show they care,
Though I can't see God, I know God's there.

Questions to Ponder: How does the wind, which we cannot see, blow?

Blow up a balloon and let out the air so the children can feel it.

Look around at the gifts of creation and know that God is here.

We do not have to *understand* God to love God. God reveals to us that love is more important than understanding or knowledge. Jesus said, "Love one another" rather than "understand one another."

The way to know God is to love God. Knowledge is loving action.

To know is to love God, for the answer is a Person. In that relationship of trust and commitment to Jesus we have the *answer*.

The first day at school, after the snacks had been distributed, the teacher closed her eyes to pray. The children followed her example, but Clara wiggled in her seat with excitement. As soon as the teacher said, "Amen," Clara exclaimed, "My mother knows God, too!"

Because children are concrete in their thinking, they imagine God in the only form they know. God is forever, therefore, God must be very old. Santa Claus is old and has a long, white beard, therefore, God must be an old man with a long, white beard, *in heaven*, sitting on a throne, for, after all, God is *boss*. Since God made rain and sun and sky, God is a *magical* old man with a long, white beard, sitting on a throne in heaven.

There is little we can do to refute the anthropomorphic image in a child's mind, but time and knowledge will correct these impressions. All of us live by symbols. The question we ask is, "What does the symbol, God, mean to the child? Does it give him or her security, trust, a sense of being loved?"

God Loves Me

Hear, O Israel: The LORD is our God, the LORD alone. You shall love the LORD your God with all your heart, and with all your soul, and with all your might. (Deut. 6:4-5)

*T*he king sought the wisest person in the kingdom, as wise as the ancient King Solomon, so he sent his messengers out into the kingdom to announce the contest. The learned wise women and men came from the east and the west, the south and the north and the king listened to their riddles, wise sayings, parables, and answers to the deepest, most mysterious, most difficult questions.

The courtyards buzzed with the words of the wise women and men and their words were carried into the courtroom and around the kingdom, for never had so many wise persons been gathered in one place. There they contested and competed with one another and when they found that their opponents were as wise as they were, they used greater volume to express their greater wisdom and the noise was deafening. The king covered his ears. His advisors covered their ears. His people covered their ears, for those proving their arguments spoke louder and louder as the day grew longer and longer.

The king asked questions and listened, until at last he cried, "Stop! I have only one more question. The one who can answer this question to my satisfaction will be acclaimed the wisest one of all and I will award that one with great riches."

Now everyone was still, for wise people know when it is best to be quiet. The king spoke his question. "Prove to me God's existence."

Philosophers, theologians, scientists, ministers, and teachers all began to speak at once, until a child within their midst whispered to the king, "Take turns."

"Take turns!" the king commanded.

For three days the king listened to their explanations, proof, affirmations of faith, to millions and billions and trillions of words, until his head was dizzy and his mind muddled.

Only the child playing on the castle floor was quiet and content.

The king was weary with wisdom and tired with tedium. He descended from his throne and joined the child on the floor, building with the blocks. "Do you believe in God?" the king asked, forgetting he was speaking to a child.

"Oh, yes," the child replied.

"How do you know?" the king asked.

"Because God loves me," the child answered, without looking up.

The king smiled. The people purred. The wise women and men murmured *their approval. The king listened to the sound of silence and breathed a sigh of relief. "Now I see, the wise one is the one who believes without reason."*

Questions to Ponder: How do you know God? How does God love you? How do you love God?

Children's questions about God are less intellectual searches for truth than emotional perplexities. Children may ask out of fear, "Can God see everything?" or curiosity, "Where does God live?" or for a need of assurance, "Why can't I see God?" or for security, "How big is God?" or for attention, "Does God like spinach?"

Children do not see, hear, or feel as adults do. To teach is to suggest to children that we have the answers and know what the child needs to know. Instead of imposing our ideas upon them, we can seek to relate to their frame of reference, to their experiences and expectations, to their needs and desires. It is speaking with commas or question marks rather than periods. In the matter of faith, commas are preferred to periods.

God's Song

This is the day that the LORD has made; let us rejoice and be glad in it. (Ps. 118:24)

Once upon a time it is said that God talked with the trees and the brooks, with the wind and the fish, and the birds and all the animals. All of them listened but they could not speak. God enjoyed the silence, listening to God's song, as God sang to them as a mother sings lullabies to her baby.

In the silence, however, God could hear God's creatures' thoughts. So one day God called them all together and said, "Just as I have given each of you one of my secrets, I am now going to give you one of my songs."

The trees, the brooks, the wind, the fish, the birds, and all the animals began to sing, each their own thanks to God. And God enjoyed their singing and their praise. Together God and creation sang.

Then God said, "Let us make a human being in our image." So God created male and female and gave them each a song to sing. The song they sang was beautiful, for together they sang with God and all creation.

With time men and women, created in the image of God, began to create. Out of their imaginations they painted the walls of their caves. Out of their imaginations they invented the wheel. Out of their imaginations they built machines to make the wheels and copies of the paintings.

94

They became so creative they had little time to sing, and with time they forgot their songs.

Like so many other things the machines did for the people, they began to sing instead. The machines sang and sang, louder and louder, until soon the people no longer heard the trees, the brooks, the wind, the fish, the birds, and all the animals.

The machines sang so loud that soon the people no longer heard God's song.

But if you are silent long enough, perhaps you may hear it whisper in the trees, the brooks, the wind, the fish, the birds, and all the animals. Perhaps you even might remember your song.

Questions to Ponder: **What did the story say to you? What is your song? Have you ever heard God's song? What would the song of God sound like?**

Sing together one of the children's favorite songs (perhaps "Jesus Loves Me" from church school).

In C. S. Lewis's *Chronicles of Narnia,* Aslan, the Lion, paced to and fro within the empty land. As he walked and sang, green grass began to grow. The grass spread out from the Lion like a pool, running up the sides of the hills like a wave. . . . Soon there were other things besides grass. Trees! In all directions the valley was swelling into humps . . . and from each hump emerged an animal.

"Narnia, Narnia, Narnia, awake. Love. Think. Speak. Be walking trees. Be talking beasts. Be divine waters." And Aslan sang his creation into being.[3]

Jesus sang a world into being through his life and death and resurrection, so that we too can sing and

> Be like the bird, who
> Halting in his flight
> On limb too slight
> Feels it give way beneath him,
> Yet sings
> Knowing he has wings.[4] And a song!

A child psychologist recently reported his experience with an eleven-year-old boy who was diagnosed as a catatonic schizophrenic. The child had not spoken in seven years. In one session with him, the therapist played Bach's "Jesus, Joy of Man's Desiring." The boy began to weep and when the music ended, he said through his tears, "That is the most powerful music I have ever heard; now I can speak!"

Crying

Jesus wept. (John 11:35 RSV)

Sometimes, no matter how I try
To stop, I can't, and have to cry.
When I fall down and skin my knee,
When my best friend is mean to me,
When I can't play and I want to,
And Mother scolds because I do.
When I am tired and quarrel and fight,
And things go wrong from morn 'til night.
Sometimes, no matter how I try
To please, I can't, and wonder "Why?"
It's then, dear God, I need to know You care.

The child was late. The mother was worried. When the child finally returned home at last, the mother anxiously asked, "What happened? What kept you so long?"

"I stopped to help a little girl who was crying over her broken doll," the child replied.

"That's nice," said her mother. "Did you help her fix her doll?"

"No, I stopped to help her cry."

Questions to Ponder: Tears are a way of "letting feelings out." Do some things make you sad? What makes you cry? What helps when we are crying? Does it help someone to cry with them?

When it seems as if the child is crying over "everything," express concern and give care. Deep emotional needs can surface through tears. A sense of insecurity or the need for a general sense of well-being may be the real cause of the tears. No child wants to feel or appear incapable.

Children who cannot cry or are teased because they cry, yet have a need to cry, are blocked from learning, from living abundantly. Children who bottle up their feelings have trouble paying attention to anything else but those feelings, even though they are doing so unconsciously. They become afraid to try, to learn, to get along with others.

Tears do not a coward make. By blocking tears, we may block other emotions as well, even those of love and affection. Studies show that people who can cry are healthier people. A spontaneous flow of tears is beneficial. Ulcers, heart trouble, asthma, and even skin eruptions may result from chronic tensions that need release.

There are times when children cry over adult decisions, for they have a right to their feelings and their tears, but adults may remain firm for the sake of the child. Adults, too, cry when they feel deeply. Through modeling concern and care for the crying child, children learn to give support to one another.

Some of us cry easily. It is the way we let our feelings out. Crying over the film, *The Last Unicorn*, three-year-old Sarah watched me and asked, "Elaine, are tears sometimes happy tears?" for I had told her that over and over so she would not be frightened by my tears. Now all I had to do was to reassure her: "Oh, yes, Sarah! Oh, yes!"

How Does God Speak to Us?

"Consider the lilies of the field, how they grow; they neither toil nor spin, yet I tell you, even Solomon in all his glory was not clothed like one of these." (Matt. 6:28-29)

I smell the perfumed rose in spring,
I hear the birds returning, sing,
I feel the gentle sun and rain,
And see the golden fields of grain.
I taste the berries ripened red,
And melons from our garden bed,
When skies above are blue and clear,
And all outdoors shouts, "God is here!"

Questions to Ponder: **How does God speak to you? How does God speak through creation?**

I may not hear God's voice or see,
Or touch God's face,
But through the love you show to me,
I know God's in this place.
I may not know the names for God,
But I can feel God's care
Through loving people who show me
That God is everywhere.

97

Questions to Ponder: **Who are the loving people in your life? How do they show you who God is?**

To understand God as creator, children need opportunities to use their senses; to play in mud, wade in water, smell, hear, see, feel, and taste.

How does God, who is Spirit, or Love, speak? I believe God speaks through the Scriptures, through prayer, through people and the events in our lives. Perhaps we do not hear God because we have learned to confine God's way of speaking by our way. Perhaps we do not hear God because we have put God so high and far away. Perhaps God is as near as the air we breathe. Perhaps God is in our breathing, in the thoughts we think, and the feelings we feel.

God is always this and that and more than this and that and other than this and that. The book of Job allows God to be God. God does not answer Job's complaints. God finally speaks, saying, "Job, look at creation!"

God's loudest voice was Jesus.

> God must be very patient
> And very, very kind,
> And very understanding
> To constantly remind
> The people of God's promise,
> "With me you will be one."
> God told them through the prophets
> Who showed what God had done.
> God even wrote a letter
> Addressed to everyone,
> But still they did not listen,
> And so God sent God's Son.

Questions to Ponder: **What is the letter called that God wrote to everyone? Why did God send God's Son?**

God's ways are not our ways, nor God's thoughts our thoughts. Did God finally wonder if we would ever understand or was it more than God could stand, so that finally God revealed through a person?

Jesus showed and taught us a new view of God that elevated and expanded former teachings about the character of God and about life lived in the presence of God, the kingdom of God.

He did this through his life and through the telling of his stories. His influence on the world reverses the world's values to understanding that the "least of these" is what matters, that love is what counts, that life is fulfilled when we pour out our lives in service to others.

The cross is a symbol of God's love because Jesus, through the cross, reversed all our values to reveal God's power and presence.

God is the Great Mystery. If God were seen or could be described, God would no longer be beyond human conception and thus less than ultimate Transcendence, but God has left us clues in Jesus, in people who love and serve, in prayer, in the church, in creation, and in God's sacred story, the Bible.

Let There Be Light

Then God said, "Let there be light"; and there was light. (Gen. 1:3)

> Perhaps God wearied of the space,
> So lonely, cold, and dark.
> Perhaps God felt a need for warmth,
> And lit a tiny spark
> That grew . . . and grew . . . and grew . . . until
> God saw what God had done.
> And with a shout God finished it,
> For God had made the sun!

Questions to Ponder: **(Read the Bible verse from your Bible.) How did God make the sun? Are there other stories of God creating?**

Words make things happen. "In the beginning God . . . said . . . and it was so. . . . " "In the beginning was the Word and the Word was with God and the Word was God."

God is the Great Word Maker.

Words are symbols of the pictures we carry in our heads. They represent (stand for) realities of things, events, visions, and feelings. For children they are magic incantations. When they say "milk," they are rewarded magically by the gift of the pure, white liquid.

To teach a child to speak words is to teach him or her to think. Stories can be vicarious experiences and powerful reinforcers. Jesus told stories because they were remembered. They were remembered because of their emotional effect.

Majestic Is Your Name!

O LORD, our Sovereign,
   how majestic is your name in all the earth! (Ps. 8:1a)

> There's splendor in the sound of it
> And music when it's said.
> It shines and sparkles on the tongue
> As starlight overhead.
> There's grandeur in the sound of it
> And dignity and might,
> And I am always dazzled by
> The glory of its light.
> There's power in the sound of it,
> And strength, as we proclaim,
> "O Lord, our Lord, of all the earth,
> Majestic is thy name!"

Questions to Ponder: **How does the poem make you feel? How do you worship God? Have you ever experienced the presence of God? What happened?**

Telling children to be reverent is different than helping them feel reverent and celebrating reverence with them. Poetry can help children experience reverence for God's name, as they join in experiencing the words.

Children need poetry that is praise, a protest against the death of hope, a search for that which will endure. Imagination and religious experience ignite the inner power that causes us to feel. The early years are the years for feeding the imagination, an opening through which faith proceeds, and that feeds religious experience. Only an exercised imagination feeds faith. When properly understood, the imagination reveals the deeper aspects of truth and reality. It supports and strengthens faith. An attentive imagination reveals and celebrates the mystery of creation, for it is the fundamental capacity to open us to the world of spirit.

Children also need real people who give hugs and hold their hands and book people who excite their imaginations and warm their hearts. Children can be fed through books, stories, poetry, and nature, so essential to their growth and spiritual development.

God's presence is with us much like the time a friend arrived to meet me, but I was so absorbed in what I was doing, I was unaware of his presence. At last he honked to get my attention and I knew he was there.

God has promised to be present. "I will be with you," but absorbed in life, I am unaware. I need awakenings, God getting my attention. I do not believe God plans pain, but I have chosen to see it and the challenges of life as opportunities for becoming aware of God.

God's presence is intangible, unseen, untouchable. When we say God is everywhere, we imply God takes up space, but God is not an object. The Spirit of God is present when we sense the wonder of people and life, worship and love.

used 10-11-98

God's Secrets

"For there is nothing hidden, except to be disclosed; nor is anything secret, except to come to light." (Mark 4:22)

There is an old story that says when a child is conceived, God whispers to that child the secrets of the universe. Then the child in the womb hears God's stories, stories of God's calling into existence the sun and moon and stars, separating the land from the waters, and creating rainbows and relationships. For nine months God reveals what there is to know of creation; then the child is ready to be born. In the excitement and joy of being born, of entering the world, however, the child forgets all the secrets, even the secret of God's love and presence; and the rest of the child's life is spent searching for those secrets once again.

Questions to Ponder: What "secret of God" did Jesus know? What is the best "secret of God" you know? (Jesus, God loves me, God is with us) If God's secrets are hidden, why are they hidden? Jesus said, "For there is nothing hidden, except to be disclosed; nor is anything secret, except to come to light." What does that mean to you?

Invite the children to engage in guided meditation. If you tell this story in sanctuary worship, invite the entire "Body of Christ" to become comfortable by placing feet on the floor, putting both hands in the lap, and closing one's eyes. Take a deep breath, slowly; now slowly let it out. Imagine you are in a favorite place where you feel comfortable and safe. (Pause.) You sense God is with you. Neither of you speak, simply enjoying being together. (Pause.) Then God whispers one of God's secrets into your ear. (Pause.) You may ask anything you need to know

101

about the secret or anything else. (Pause.) Then when you are ready, return to this place, and open your eyes.

Trusting God

"And even the hairs of your head are all counted." (Matt. 10:30)

*H*e *was four and life was full of friends, and fun, and frustration! Today he had had a fight with his favorite friend. It hurt, so he cried and came home to find comfort.*

As he sat on his father's lap, his father comforted him. "It will be all right. You will be friends again. The hurt will go away."

The boy wore a cap and held his head and continued to cry.

"I know it hurts," his father said, feeling the sadness of a broken friendship, while the child continued to cry softly.

"Do you want me to kiss the hurt away?" his father asked. It was a game they played.

The boy shook his head "no."

"Do you want me to call Billy?"

Again the boy shook his head "no." "It doesn't hurt," he sobbed.

The father was surprised and then, at last, silent. Perhaps he would listen rather than talk. So he asked, "Why are you crying then?"

The boy removed his cap and his hand from his head to show his father, as he said, "Billy pulled out my hair and now God will have to count them all over again!"

Questions to Ponder: Have you ever been hurt by a friend's word or action? How did it feel? What did you do? What does Jesus tell us about God in the Bible verse? What do you learn about God from the story?

Trust is the willingness to believe until we can know. The "facts" we give the child today may be obsolete by tomorrow, but the way children learn for themselves, the confidence and joy they experience in learning for themselves, will last a lifetime. "Give learners a fish and you feed them for today. Teach them how to fish, and you feed their tomorrows."

The greatest gift we can give a child is to model trust. Trust in God, faith, comes to and through the child as we share with one another our love of God and God's love for us. Children can show us how to trust

God, and because we cannot do the deed, deserve the desire, or goal the gift, we accept God's grace with wonder and gratitude.

Trust is built on love, but we do not learn love in the abstract. Children need experiences of love before they can understand the words, "God loves you."

> Trust grows slowly, like a tree,
> Strong and sturdy, steadily,
> Stretching leaves and limbs above,
> As arms that hold us in their love.
> Everyone needs trust to grow,
> Deep roots of faith so they may know
> And show . . . trust.

In spite of life's vulnerability, our prayer is that all children learn to trust life, trust themselves, and trust others.

Where Is God?

9.20.98
MPC - Dayton

*W*here is God?" the child asked, as she sat down to breakfast one morning.

Mother dried her hands and sat down at the table with Susan. She had not thought about how she would answer her child when the question was asked and being mortal and finite she did not presume to know all about God. She believed God was Spirit and was everywhere. She believed also that in some way God was Parent. It would have been easiest to say "God is in heaven," but she knew her child would look up into the sky. She did not want to confine God to a particular place. If she said, "God is everywhere," Susan was sure to ask, "In the oven? In my shoe? In Daddy's ear?" It was not an easy question to answer.

Finally the mother sighed, saying, "God is within you. God helps you love."

Susan was silent. She looked down at the cereal she was eating and took another spoonful, chewing it slowly, as she mumbled, "Watch out, God, here it comes!"

Questions to Ponder: Have you ever wondered "Where is God?" Where do you think God is?

"Where is God?" an adult asked the five-year-old, and the child replied, "Where isn't God?"

Some people say "God is in heaven."

I used to wonder,
When I was seven,
Where is the place
Adults call "heaven"?
But I've discovered
Now that I'm eleven,
Wherever God is,
That is heaven.

Many children want to know "Where is heaven?" How we answer helps determine whether children see God as One who loves, as the three-year-old who from time to time would look at the sky and say to God, calling, "Hey, Mom, God's looking at me!" or the One who "spies." "God, go away," said the angry six-year-old.

A group of learned rabbis came to a rabbi who was renowned for his wisdom, and together they learned from one another. At one point the rabbi asked the wise men, "Where is the dwelling of God?"

They looked surprised and stretched out their arms to indicate all the earth, when the rabbi answered his own question, "The dwelling of God is wherever we let God in."

We stutter before the mystery of God and God's creation. God's ways are not our ways. Then how can we explain with frail words? Poetry and parables express concerns, conviction, and commitments, for they speak to our hearts, as well as our heads. Poetry and parables care for the soul.

We use metaphors to expand and describe our thinking. A man, officially retired, spent twelve hours each day either calling on church members or counseling them in a tiny room in the church. The room was barely big enough for a desk and chair for his visitors. One day he enthusiastically told a small girl what it meant for him to be a Christian. Throwing his arms wide, in a gesture to indicate the Christian community around the world, he said, "This is the kingdom of heaven."

Weeks later the young girl told her friend about the kingdom of heaven: "It is really a wonderful place. It has only one window and everyone has to stand up, but it's lovely there."

104

Celebrating Lent: The Season of the Sacred Story

Lent is the season of the sacred story of Jesus' suffering, death, and resurrection. Children are confused by the death of their friend. We can help them understand that it was the consequences of his brave and trusting actions and parables.

Jesus told parables of reversal: the one who showed mercy to the wounded man on the road was not a priest or one of God's chosen people, but was . . . surprise . . . the enemy! The one who came into the workplace last received . . . surprise . . . the same as the "early bird." The one who deserted his father, squandered his money, and frequented the wrong company was . . . surprise . . . welcomed home with a feast. Jesus was a friend to a woman. As if being a woman was not bad enough, she was a Samaritan woman, a woman belonging to the enemy nation. Jesus was a friend to Zacchaeus who cheated, and to a woman of the city who was a sinner. Jesus strangely called us to such a risk, for in the reversal is revelation.

God took the symbol of humanity's cruelty, the cross, and transformed it into the symbol of God's love.

Spiritual reality is expressed in symbols. Symbolical language is the language of inner experience, thoughts, and feelings expressed as if they were sensory events in the external world. Symbols are nonthreatening because they "whisper," suggest, or nudge. W. H. Auden, the poet, said that you cannot tell people what to do. You can only tell them parables, and parables are symbolical.

When my children were young and "lost" a word or had not found one yet, they created their own, usually one that enlarged its reality concretely through sound or sight. Perhaps, as children in the spirit, without the words we need to communicate, we should be more interested in the experience, creating our own words for and from it. Perhaps "talking in tongues" is experiencing the power of the words rather than their meaning.

We stutter in symbol, mutter in metaphor, and praise in parable. Symbol is our safeguard against being too familiar or too incorrect, making God an "object" in time and space, as well as expressing the depth and wonder of the mystery of the cross.

Reversal of our normal expectations is revelation and it is true that the most profound and shocking reversal is that of God on a cross. In the midst of his pain and humiliation Jesus continued to love, for God is love. Jesus revealed that love. That God should endure pain is a reversal of religious experience.

Palm Sunday

Based on Mark 11:1-11.

Nathaniel's colt had no name. At first Nathaniel called him "Faithful," then "Long Ears," then "Flash," but none of the names seemed to fit his colt.

He was sorry his colt did not have a name because he loved him. Nathaniel never rode him because the colt was his pet. He wanted to wait until the colt was older and Nathaniel would not be such a burden on him.

Nathaniel was thinking of his colt as he walked the dusty road and met the stranger. The stranger introduced himself, saying, "My name is Jesus. My friends and I are on our way to Jerusalem. We are looking for a colt. Would you know of any I could borrow?"

Nathaniel thought of his colt, but his colt had never been ridden. Nathaniel shook his head. "I do not know for sure, but I will ask my father."

"I only wish to borrow it," Jesus repeated.

Nathaniel thought about the colt and the man the rest of the way home.The next day, on his way to the village, he saw a crowd of people on the hillside. Nathaniel decided to stop.

The people were listening carefully to the man who was teaching. It was the stranger, Jesus! He was teaching the people about God's kingdom and God's love for all people.

When Jesus' friends came to Nathaniel's house the next day to ask to borrow Nathaniel's colt, he gave it to them gladly, and when Nathaniel saw Jesus riding on his colt, he was so pleased.

Nathaniel followed Jesus and his colt. When the people along the road saw

Jesus riding the colt, they cried, "Hosanna! Blessed is the one who comes in the name of the Lord!"

Nathaniel too shouted with joy, "Hosanna!" which means "save us." When the procession was over, Nathaniel went up to Jesus. Jesus thanked him for the use of his colt and asked, "What is your colt's name?"

Nathaniel looked at Jesus. He thought about the happy shouts and his nameless colt. "Hosanna!" he replied joyously.

Jesus waved Nathaniel and Hosanna out of sight down the dusty road back to Nathaniel's village. "I wonder where he's going next?" Nathaniel said to Hosanna, as the colt nuzzled the neck of his friend.

Questions to Ponder: **Do you have a pet? If Jesus asked to borrow it, would you give it to Jesus? Why? What does "Hosanna" mean?**

(Palm Sunday is a joyous occasion. Give each child a branch and lead them down the center aisle back to their individual pews.)

Young children will not understand all of Lent but they can begin to participate in it. When my friend, Charles, was five years old he made pretzels in his church school class during Lent. Driving home, I asked him, "Charles, do you know why you made pretzels today?" He shook his head. "Long ago when people prayed to God, they placed their arms over their chests, their hands on their shoulders in a way that looked like a pretzel. Whenever they saw a pretzel, it reminded them of God who provides food for our bodies. So we make pretzels during Lent, the time of the year when we think about Jesus and God and prayer, for pretzels are twisted the way people used to cross their arms in prayer," I explained. There was silence. There were no questions. Did he understand? I waited, but there was nothing but silence. At last I asked, "Charles, what is Lent?" to which he replied, "Lent is the time pretzels pray to God."

Children think both concretely and imaginatively.

Anna's Fire

"You shall love your neighbor as yourself." (Mark 12:31)

I will build the biggest and best bonfire this year, Karl," Anna announced to her brother. Karl was older and therefore, according to Karl, could do anything "better."

Tomorrow would be the first Sunday of Lent. In Belgium, where Anna and

Karl lived, it was called the "Sunday of the Great Fires." Today Anna and Karl would go from house to house begging wood to build their fires. Whoever made the largest fire would win and be the "luckiest" person for the rest of the year.

"Anna, you are a girl. You cannot burn a bigger bonfire than the one I will build," Karl explained to his sister.

"I have been building the fires for Mother to bake all this year. You will see," Anna answered.

"You do not understand. The more wood one can gather and carry, the bigger the bonfire. You cannot carry as much wood as I, for the wood is heavy."

Anna did not explain to her brother how hard she had worked that year while Mother had been ill. "I am strong," she told herself. "I want to be 'lucky.' "

There were many reasons why Anna wanted to be the "luckiest," but the most important reason was to make her mother happy. Anna's mother had been ill and sad for so long that Anna wanted to win for her mother's sake.

"I will not take sides," Mother declared, listening to Anna and Karl. "Perhaps you will both win. Perhaps there will be a tie."

"No tie!" called Karl over his shoulder, as he left to gather wood.

"No tie," repeated Anna, giving her mother a final hug before she left to gather wood for her bonfire.

All day the children gathered wood, knocking on the doors of their village friends. Anna worked hard and long and hid her wood where Karl would not find it. Tomorrow night she would burn the brighest fire she had ever burned!

Anna could hardly sleep that night because of her fatigue from her excitement and from carrying the wood, but the next morning she was refreshed and ready to begin.

Anna found a cardboard box in which she placed the heavy wood. With a piece of rope she made a handle to pull the box. This way she could drag the wood up the mountain.

In her excitement Anna asked her mother if she could leave early that afternoon, and her mother, smiling, replied that she would do the same, for it would take her longer than the others to walk up the mountain. "But go on ahead, Anna, and God bless you."

Anna waited until Karl was gone and then raced to her hiding place. "I have been lucky already," she thought, dragging the heavy box behind her.

It was a long walk up the mountain over the stones and rocks scattered along the way. As the mountain became steeper, the box became heavier. Once Anna even wondered if Karl had been right, a girl was not as strong as a boy. "I am just as determined, however," Anna assured herself.

Halfway up the mountain, Anna's luck ran out. "Oh, no!" she cried. The stones had torn and broken the bottom of the cardboard box and Anna's wood lay scattered along the side of the road.

108

Quickly gathering the heavy wood, Anna loaded it in her arms. "I will have to make several trips," she moaned to herself, under the heavy load of wood in her arms. "But I was lucky to have begun early," she added.

It was late that afternoon when Anna carried her last piece of wood to the mountaintop. The others had begun to arrive, all carrying wood for their fires. The sun was setting and soon bonfires would brighten the mountaintop, and one bonfire would burn the brightest!

Anna smiled within, as she sighed. Then she heard the cry. Anna looked up from her pile of wood to see Bertha standing beside her. Bertha was her friend. "What is the matter, Bertha?" she asked, looking down at her small friend.

Tears flowed down the cheeks of the small child, as she sobbed her story to Anna. "I have no wood for a bonfire, Anna. Someone stole the wood I had gathered."

Anna looked at her friend and knew just how she was feeling. It was an old superstition that if one did not build a bonfire, they would have "bad luck" that year. "I came up the mountain to borrow some wood but no one will share any of their wood," Bertha continued.

Anna looked at the large pile of wood she had gathered and carried up the long, steep climb. She remembered how hard she had worked all that year to be strong enough so that her bonfire would burn the brightest. "I have enough wood for both of us, Bertha," she replied.

That night the bonfires blazed brightly on the mountaintop, celebrating the first Sunday of Lent, to remember Christ is the "light" of the world. Anna knew she would not win that year, but seeing Bertha's smiling face in the light of her bonfire, Anna already felt as if she were the luckiest one.

"Anna," said a voice in the darkness.

"Mother! I did not know you were here yet!"

"I was walking slowly behind you all the way up the mountain and I saw what you did for Bertha. You have made me the happiest mother in the world!"

"Oh, Mother," Anna cried, nestling in her mother's arms as they watched the fires burn.

One fire burned more brightly than all the rest that night. Karl's fire had won again, but the feeling in Anna's heart burned even brighter than Karl's fire.

Questions to Ponder: Why did Anna want to win? Do you think she did? What did Anna win? The contest took place on the first Sunday in Lent. What relationship to Lent are fires? What does Lent mean to you?

It is said that God creates stories to plant seeds of hope in order to help birth a faith into bloom under the bright sunlight of God's love.

Stories feed our imaginations, our feelings, and our intuition. They suggest and describe rather than define.

Lent is a time for remembering sacred stories. We remember the stories of Jesus' happy entrance into Jerusalem on Palm Sunday, of his Last Supper with his friends, of his trials before Annas and Pilate, the horror of crucifixion, and the glorious resurrection.

Christ's Resurrection

"Do not be alarmed; you are looking for Jesus of Nazareth, who was crucified. He has been raised; he is not here." (Mark 16:6)

> The cherry and the apple,
> The pear are now in bloom,
> Sweeping away the cobwebs
> Of winter's weary gloom,
> Spring's way of recognizing
> Christ's resurrection from the tomb.

Questions to Ponder: The story of Easter is the story of "resurrection." What do you see, feel, and think, when you hear the word "resurrection"?

Most children think of bunnies and Easter eggs. Adults see new, fresh, clean clothes or "beings." Some see new buds on the trees about to burst into bloom, or butterflies emerging from confining cocoons. Still others see forgiveness from confining guilt, a new chance to begin again, or Jesus in the garden with Mary, calling her name. There are those who see "a new heaven and a new earth," where God wipes away the tears and there is no mourning. But there are also those who see nothing, whose pain or doubt is so great it replaces all images of hope. For me, the image of resurrection is hope in a new beginning.

Early Sunday Morning

Based on 1 Corinthians 15:35-38.

> Early Sunday morning
> Wrapped in grief and gloom

Friends of Jesus hurried
And found an empty tomb.
Death could not destroy him,
God had had God's way.
Because Christ lives forever,
We celebrate today!

Questions to Ponder: **What is today? What is special about today? How do you celebrate?**

Children will not be afraid of life if the adults around them are not afraid of death. During Lent four-year-old Jonathan gathered the cardboard blocks into the center of the room and placed them into the form of a cross. Jonathan then lay down on the blocks, stretching his arms from his sides. Jonathan was trying on and trying out what he had seen or heard.

Resurrection is the realization of God's love remaking us into a new being, destroying everything that is against love, and thus we are reunited with life. When we are accepted by God, we can love others without reward, the answering love of the other. When we are accepted by God, we can love ourselves. Being forgiven is accepting oneself.

Forget Me Not

Based on Mark 15:37-39.

*T*he *sounds of "hosannas" rang in his ears. How the people had praised him! Now Jesus thought, "How quickly they forget!" For Jesus had just discovered that one of his disciples had made a deal with the chief priests to betray him for thirty pieces of silver.*

"How could Judas forget so quickly!" Jesus thought. Learning the news, Jesus walked quietly to the small garden outside the walls of the city of Jerusalem. It was here he went to talk with God, where he could be away from everyone and be alone with God.

"Father, how quickly they forget!" Jesus said.

Jesus frequently spent time alone in the Garden of Gethsemane in prayer, but today he stayed longer than usual.

"Thy will be done. Amen." At last Jesus stood up and listened to the song of the bird that was singing above his head. He felt the warm sun on his arms. The Garden was alive with sound and color.

As Jesus walked toward the gate, he smelled the wildflowers and enjoyed their

111

fragrance. "What is this?" he asked suddenly, seeing a tiny blue flower nestled among the tall green grass. "What are you called?" he asked aloud.

"Master, I have no name, for I am the forgotten one."

The memory of the words flooded over Jesus. He recalled the words he had spoken earlier in the morning. He remembered his bitter disappointment in his friend. "Yes, how quickly one is forgotten," he agreed. Then Jesus smiled and whispered to the small blue flower. "Forget me not!"

From that day the small blue flower became the symbol of true love, which never forgets the loved one, the Master of Gethsemane.

Questions to Ponder: **What reminds you of Jesus? Why was Jesus sad? Where do you pray?**

In *Story Journey* Tom Boomershine tells Richard Rice's story of his congregation's "forget-me-not," their remembrance of the story:

"Our group began meeting about eight weeks before Easter. After the first meetings, we agreed that one person in the group would learn the story and tell it in worship for the Scripture lesson each week during Lent. . . .

"The response of the congregation to the telling of the stories was extremely positive, which provided a high degree of incentive for the group. People were excited to see other lay persons telling the stories from memory. They also found the lessons more alive which in turn helped my preaching. . . .

"Sometime around the middle of Lent, I proposed to the group that we would tell the entire passion narrative for the Good Friday service. At first, people were reluctant and thoroughly frightened. But when I made it clear that they would only have to tell the stories they had already learned and I would do the rest, they were finally more than willing to do it.

"On Good Friday, we rearranged the pews so that the congregation was gathered around us in a rough semi-circle with the group seated on a bench facing them. We began by singing two passion hymns and then we simply told the story. There were two other hymns during the telling of the story. As the story progressed, the congregation became more and more deeply involved. By the end there was a primary sense of the holiness and the reality of Jesus' death. It was the most meaningful Good Friday service we have ever had. The people were so appreciative and asked that we tell the story every year.

"This experience has made me aware of the power of the story when it is simply told. No sermon could have been more powerful than that story. And the people who told the story have become far more committed leaders in the life of the congregation. Telling the story changed them. It is clear to me that telling the biblical stories introduces a whole new element of meaning that has simply not been present before in the way we have used the Scriptures."[1]

The Dogwood

Whatever is true, . . . think about these things. (Phil. 4:8)

> Whatever is true, is beautiful,
> Think on these things,
> The dogwood blossom in the spring
> That blooms as gently as God's care
> For those who need, the ones who have not,
> The ones who share.
> And though it blooms for such a little while,
> Its grace redeems the commonplace and
> Nothing is the same again.
> How strange to choose a bloom so delicate
> To symbolize the cruelty of our human race.
> The dogwood is the paradox
> That makes us wise.

Once upon a time the tiny, delicate dogwood tree was a tall, sturdy, and strong tree. Then something terrible happened. "Which tree shall we choose?" asked the man with the axe.

"It must be strong," was the reply.

"This tree looks good to me." The man with the axe pointed to the dogwood tree.

"That's the tree," the other agreed.

The sharp axe blade cut into the bark of the dogwood tree. But the tree was strong and sturdy and ready, for it had always known that someday it would be cut down. That was its purpose for growing strong and sturdy. The tree, however, did not know how it was to be used.

"It will make a good cross for the carpenter of Nazareth to die upon," said the man with the axe.

The tree did not know what a "cross" was. Now it eagerly looked forward to the day that it would become a cross. One of its cousins had become a table and one had become a chair. But none of them had ever been a cross.

"I am going to be a cross," thought the dogwood tree, as it was lifted into the

113

air and carried into the city. There it was made into a cross and put on the back of a man wearing a crown of thorns on his head. The tree tried to be as light as it could be, but it was a large, heavy tree. "I am sorry, Master," the tree-cross whispered to the carpenter of Nazareth. "I am sorry to be so heavy on your back."

"I am carrying a heavier burden than you, dear tree," the man replied, trying to comfort the dogwood tree.

But the tree in the form of a cross was so heavy it was hard for the man to talk, so the dogwood was silent.

When the man reached the place called Golgotha, the tree-cross was pounded into the ground. The dogwood wondered why, but said nothing. It was not until he felt them nailing the man to his cross that he cried, "Oh, Master, how cruel! How cruel that I should be used this way, that I should be part of your pain. Forgive me, Master, forgive me."

Again the man tried to comfort the dogwood. But the dogwood was too sad. "Listen to me," the man said at last. "Because you care so much, you will never be used this way again. Instead, from this day, you shall be small and thin and twisted."

It happened as the man promised. Today the dogwood tree is small and thin and twisted and each dogwood blossom is in the form of a cross with a crown of thorns in the center.

Questions to Ponder: What happened to the dogwood tree?

Show the "print of thorns" in the dogwood blossom.

Lent is a time to help children have confidence that God cares and is there to strengthen and guide when they are coping with sadness or loss. Praying together, teaching children to meditate by being silent and listening, and reading the Bible can support the child's belief that God loves us and is always with us.

If children are old enough to write, journaling is an important way to express feelings. Younger children work through traumatic events by reliving them in an imaginative way through play. Books and stories invite such play and release talk.

Will I Die?

Not one bird falls to the ground apart from God. (Matt. 10:29 paraphrased)

The four-year-old climbed up into my lap, asking, "Will I die?"

I replaced the sewing in my lap with the child, wondering what I would say. Slowly, stumbling, I explained God's love and plan for life and death, my hope and trust in God. He nestled in my lap, my arms around him making him feel safe. He listened, although he did not understand, and when I stopped talking at last, he looked up and smiled. "I only wanted to know if I had time for another cookie."

Questions to Ponder: **Has anyone you know died? Have you ever wondered, "Will I die?" Death is a part of life. We all die.**

We chuckle at the logic of a young child. We laugh with relief, because we have been relieved of "explaining" a mystery, the mystery of death. We giggle nervously because we too are small children, questioning our loving Parent. "Will I die?"

Death is a reality. It is the most difficult subject for postmodern women and men to discuss. Whenever I hear people say, "I lost . . . ," the child in me wants to ask, "Where did you lose them?"

Young children want to know why their pet died. Maybe its life was over. "Why?" Maybe it had finished living. Maybe it was time for a new challenge, a new change. Maybe I don't know.

"What happens after we die?"

"I do not know." Because we are encountering mystery, it is permissible to reply, "I do not know."

When all else fails (but not as the easy way out), you may have to say "I do not know." It is all right not to know the answer. Not knowing keeps us human and humble. It invites our imaginations to express our faith. Faith does not have all the answers but faith trusts the One who does. It also invites us to invite our children to think for themselves, to use their imaginations, to bring asker and answerer together to struggle with the deeper issues of our faith, the mysteries of our encounters and dialogues with God. Theology is not simple. Life is not a series of questions to be answered, problems to be solved, but a celebration, an act of praise to God who loves us and gives us life. It is a service of joy to God's incarnation among us.

Death is a part of life. If children do not experience death directly, through the loss of a pet or a person, they see it daily on television or in the newspaper.

About age four, sometimes before, children begin to ask questions about the natural world (What makes the clouds? How are babies born? Who made the world?), and questions about life and death (Why did

Grandma die? What is death? Where is heaven? Who is God? Does God love me?).

The child's first reaction to death is "Fix it, Mommy, Daddy." This may be the child's first encounter with the fact that his parents are not omnipotent, that some of the experiences of life are mysteries and unfixable.

From age three to five children deny death. "Bang! Bang! You're dead. Now get up. It's my turn!" Death is like a sleep from which the person will awaken in the morning. At this age they have difficulty differentiating between animate and inanimate things. They become angry at the table leg they bump. "You bad leg!" Death is reversible, an abstract concept, outside of their experience.

Between ages five and nine children personify death, not yet accepting its finality. After age nine children recognize death as inevitable to all persons. How one answers the questions, "What happens when people die?" "Why do they die?" and "Where do they go?" depends upon the age and interest of the child.

"Why did she or he die?" is a normal question. Some children are ready for a factual explanation: "The body stopped breathing. The body was worn out and unable to function so the heart stopped beating."

Accidents, disease, war, and old age are the four common causes of death.

It is important to answer a child's questions about death, but it is wise to avoid using euphemisms because of the confusion and fear they cause in the minds of children: "Mother went on a 'journey.' " "Grandpa went 'to sleep' and 'passed on.' " "God wanted Aunt Jo to live with him in heaven." "God needed Daddy."

It is the child who needs Daddy. A "journey" is not the end of life, but may be the beginning. To sleep is safe. And Easter is to celebrate!

Engaging in Love

Children express love in unique ways. I have a friend whose name is Sarah. She is now fourteen, but when she was five, and we were driving in the car, Sarah said, "Elaine, are you going to die before I do?"

I replied, "I hope so."

"Why?" she asked.

"So you can live longer."

Then Sarah replied, "I wish you had been born when I was."

"Thank you, Sarah."

"Because I want you to live as long as I do!"

There is nothing like the love of a child. When children receive love, they give love in return. Sarah was loved and because she was loved, Sarah loved.

We were enjoying the circus when suddenly I had a fit of shivers, and a sudden attack of flu. By the time we reached Sarah's house, I could only fall onto the couch. Sarah, then three years old, covered me with her constant companion, her blanket, and then her Little-Bit (her cat), as her gesture of concern.

Sarah, the imaginative one, the lover. "Sarah, what do you think?" I asked, as we looked up at the star-filled sky, when she was five.

"I think the Emperor of the Earth loves us very much."

A Gift of Love

"I came that they may have life, and have it abundantly." (John 10:10)

*L*ook what I painted for you! It's a beautiful painting!" Carrie called to her mother at the end of the church school hour.

117

It had dots of red and green and yellow blended together. In some places there were blotches of brown. Carrie had painted the picture with joy and love. She had painted the picture for her mother all by herself, so to Carrie it was a beautiful painting.

No one knew what she was thinking as she painted, because it was her own painting. No one knew what she was feeling while she painted, because it was her own painting.

It was her painting for her mother. And when she gave the yellow, green, red, and brown painting, her mother saw the smile of happiness on Carrie's face. "I did it for you because I love you, Mommy!"

Mother listened to Carrie's words and hugged her daughter. "Thank you, Carrie. It is a beautiful painting!"

The painting was given with joy and received with joy. It was a painting of love. It was part of a relationship of love. It was, indeed, a beautiful painting.

Questions to Ponder: **What did Carrie give her mother? Why? How do you show love and compassion?**

Pray: "Thank you, God, for love, the greatest force on earth. Amen."

The child walked over to the neighbor's house to visit the family whose father had died. She had watched her mother prepare food to share with them. Without being told to do it, the child had picked a flower from her own garden, put it in a vase, and now took it to the wife, saying, "I love you."

The woman later said that that expression of love was the most meaningful act she received during her sorrow.

Social ethics for children include compassion, gifts of love, care for others and for creation, care for people who are like me and you and for people who are different, care for those who are less fortunate than we are in monetary and physical possessions and for those who are more fortunate than us, perhaps, in the way they love and are loved.

Some families have many physical possessions and few precious times together. Other people have few physical possessions but are "rich" in other ways. Social ethics is the way we treat *all* people.

How do children learn to love? A woman who grew up in the South before the Civil Rights Movement learned what her culture taught her, but she also learned the song, "Jesus loves the little children, all the children of the world. Red, brown, yellow, black and white, they are precious in his sight, Jesus loves the little children of the world" that her church taught her. If Jesus loved the black children, could she do less?

118

Singing those words Sunday after Sunday changed her whole way of being.

When children experience giving and receiving love, they begin to understand what it means to love. Experience comes before knowledge.

Goodness

Beloved, let us love one another, because love is from God; everyone who loves is born of God and knows God. (1 John 4:7)

Sometimes he was good. Sometimes he was not. Although he was only three years old, he knew the difference, and one day Buzz was upset. He was angry. "If somebody wanted me, would you give me away?" he asked his mother.

"No," his mother assured him.

"Why?" Buzz wanted to know.

"We could never give you away because we love you," his mother replied.

"Yes, you love me because I share."

His mother gathered Buzz in her arms. "We love you because you are you. We would love you even if you did not share, but we are glad that you do share."

There was a big sigh from such a small boy.

Questions to Ponder: Have you ever wondered if you were loved when you made a mistake or hurt someone? God loves us all the time. We are never away from God's love.

It is easy to love a good child, but the good news of the gospel assures us that God loves the good and the bad, the just and the unjust, that God loves us even when we have done nothing to deserve God's love. We accept this gift freely, not because of who we are, but because of who God is.

Children develop the roots of self-confidence and faith when the adults in their world accept and support them as they are. Sometimes children feel that they are only loved when they are "good," when they perform according to the adults' expectations.

In an atmosphere of trust, children may reveal their understandings and interpretations. "Be good! God knows whatever you do" threatens children to react in much the same way as two girls who were digging a hole beside the path on their way to school. Seeing an adult approaching them, they quickly covered the hole. "What are you doing?" the adult asked the girls. The girls looked at each other, each wondering what the other's response would be. At last one of them exclaimed in an excited voice, "We buried God! We didn't want God with us today!"

"Roots" include both self-confidence and self-control, so we both love and discipline children. We can, however, value children's initiative in self-assertion even when we must stop or prohibit inappropriate behavior. In developing roots children can be given opportunities for making choices and for becoming responsible for their choices and their consequences within limits.

Developing roots of faith means giving children love, security, and trust out of one's own relationship of love, security, and trust in God.

Experiencing love is a learning that lasts for a lifetime, a learning that enriches and makes the living of life meaningful. The mother hugged her four-year-old son. "Charles," she said, "I hope we will always be friends, even when you grow up."

And the child replied, "Even when my feet grow long, Mommie, we'll still be friends."

A Suit of Armor

Jesus said, "Put your sword back into its place; for all who take the sword will perish by the sword." (Matt. 26:52)

*O*nce upon a time in the land of Noil there lived a giant ogre. He was the meanest, ugliest, fiercest ogre people had ever seen or heard or even imagined. All the ogre had to do was roar and the people would run and hide for weeks.

Brave knights put on their armor and went out to fight the ogre. How they rattled when the ogre lifted them above his head as easily as toothpicks and threw them to the ground!

Shy Sylvester had heard the ogre, too, and when he did, he dug a deep hole in the ground and hid, because he had no armor. He had no armor because shy Sylvester was too shy to fight.

Because he was so shy everything went wrong for Sylvester. He always seemed to be shaking and spilling and tripping, and everyone laughed and made fun of Sylvester.

"Sylvester, why don't you go and fight the ogre?" Laura the Lovely asked one day.

"I haven't any armor," he replied, shyly.

"My Uncle Evert's armor is set up in the castle," said Lovely Laura. "I will

get it for you. Then when you have fought the ogre, I will return it to the castle."

Shy Sylvester did not want to fight the ogre. He didn't think that he was afraid, but he knew he was shy, too shy to tell Lovely Laura, for he knew she would only laugh. Everyone laughed at Sylvester and this only made him more shy. But before he knew what was happening, he was dressed in Uncle Evert's knight's armor.

"You look handsome!" Lovely Laura exclaimed.

Shy Sylvester was glad that Lovely Laura could not see him blush. Yet he did feel brave. But in his hurry and inexperience in wearing heavy armor, Sylvester tripped on the first step and clattered down the stairway of the castle.

Lovely Laura filled the castle halls with her laughter and Sylvester turned as red as a summer rose. "I am going home," he whispered, as Lovely Laura helped him to his feet.

"Oh, no!" she cried. "Sylvester, you are the bravest."

In bravery, as in fear, things happen before one is aware, and Sylvester, without knowing how, was suddenly facing the ogre. In that moment there was no time for fear or bravery as he watched the ogre pulling up trees and chewing boulders.

Sylvester wondered why he was here. He had never liked fighting and here he was fighting a monster who would destroy him.

"I'm glad you've come," the ogre roared. "If you had not come to me, I was going to come to you and destroy all the people in your village. Now I have something better to do," he said, picking Sylvester up with two fingers and dropping him on the ground.

Sylvester struggled to rise but the aged armor locked and he could not move. There he stood, shaking like a puppy, as the ground shook with him, for the ogre was laughing with such might that the land jiggled as jelly. The ogre clapped his hands on his stomach and rolled on the ground shaking with laughter.

Sylvester was used to people laughing at him, but never an ogre!

"This is more fun than fighting!" the ogre shouted. "I haven't laughed this much in forty years. Rusty, you are a riot!"

The ogre slapped Sylvester on the back and the ancient armor squeaked and unlocked. Sylvester went sprawling onto the ground, but the ogre only laughed harder. "If you will visit me once a month so that I may laugh, I promise I will never fight again," the ogre said.

Sylvester agreed, thinking, "It's better to laugh than fight." So Sylvester returned the ancient armor to the ancient castle, for he no longer needed this ancient way of winning.

Questions to Ponder: What did the story say to you? Have you ever had to face a problem like Sylvester's? What did you do? Is it better

to laugh or fight? What did Jesus mean about those who "take" the sword shall perish [die] by the sword?

Give each child a flower. "I have heard that when one eats a flower, one will never be violent again. As we pretend to eat a petal, let us close our eyes and thank God for the peace that passes all understanding."

Fantasy, springing from the deepest inspiration, can present courage and possibility against impossible odds and comfort for disappointments and disillusionments. Though it may not be "factual," fantasy can heal because it is true to the heart, the intuition, the imagination. Because fantasies do not deal directly with the concrete world, they are free of limitations.

A boring speaker lectured on and on for an hour and a half. A highly gifted, imaginative student sat there listening, his eyes shining, a gentle smile crossing his face. "It was so wonderful when the bear jumped into the water," he said at the close of the talk. He had chosen an alternative use for his energies. Through his imagination he left the auditorium and the audience for a happier place.

Children are not disturbed by mystery or paradox. Our literal, logical "answers" disappear as mist before the rising sun, as the mythical creatures open the doors of inner magic.

Albert Einstein knew that the source of wonder, the ability to appreciate the concrete, particular, unique gifts of creation, was the imagination. Once, when he was asked to explain the theory of relativity in simple terms, he replied, "I cannot do it, but call on me at Princeton and I will play it for you on my violin."

In George Bernard Shaw's play *Joan of Arc* her tormenters taunt her, "You say that God speaks to you. That is only your imagination." And Joan replies, "Yes, that is the way God speaks to me."

Accidents

Train up a child in the way he should go,
and when he is old he will not depart from it. (Prov. 22:6 RSV)

*J*immie *wanted to help. Without asking the teacher whether she needed help, Jimmie carried the jars of paint across the room. Suddenly he slipped and the jars crashed into tiny pieces as they hit the tile floor with yellow paint flying, pouring, bouncing into large puddles of paint.*

The teacher closed her eyes and groaned inwardly. She wanted to say, "Why can't you be more careful?" Instead she went to Jimmie and put her arms around him. Then turning him around, still in her arms, to face the paint, she said, "It's all right, Jimmie. See the beautiful painting it made!"

Stunned. Afraid. Cringing in expectation of scolding and punishment, Jimmie and the other children relaxed, stood, looked, and talked. But not for long, for soon the paint would stain and get tracked around the room. With mop and bucket, Jimmie cleaned up the mess he had made, but not before he and the other children had learned that accidents mean something is being done.

Questions to Ponder: Have you ever had an accident? What happened? How did you feel? Is there a difference between accidents and doing something on purpose? Did Jimmie mean to fall and break the jars of paint? What is forgiveness? What is love? Who gives you love?

For older children tell the story of Peter and his denial of Jesus (Mark 14:66-72). Children prefer hearing to reading a story.

The young child came crying to his teacher. He was holding his head, and the teacher put the child on his lap. "Did you have an accident?" he asked, comforting the child.

The child trusted his teacher. He felt safe and loved in his lap and he stopped crying to reply, "Christopher hit me, but I'd like to think it was an accident, because he's my best friend."

All people have accidents, grown-ups and children. A very distinguished, dignified man, a doctor, one evening sat at the dinner table of his friends as an invited guest. *Accidentally,* he spilled his coffee on the pure white tablecloth, his face flushed with embarrassment.

The hostess, the woman who had prepared the dinner, saw how he felt and said, "I like that color," as she turned over her coffee cup, watching the rich, brown liquid streaming over the white tablecloth.

Her husband said, "I do, too" and turned over his cup, turning an accident into a most delightful occasion.

Correction and instruction with love are means of growth. A calm explanation, a just but not harsh consequence, and the knowledge that repetition and consistency will be necessary on the part of the adult, will provide children with the best conditions for learning.

CT 5.28.00

bulldog 16.3

usedDT
11.26.17

X the
King

used
5.28.00
MPC

Love in a Lunchbox

Love in the Heart

"And the king will answer them, 'Truly I tell you, just as you did it to one of the least of these who are members of my family, you did it to me.' " (Matt. 25:40)

A king who had no sons sent out his messengers to announce that every young man might apply for an interview with the king to be the next king, if they did the following two things:

1. They must love God and

2. they must love others.

One young man indeed loved God and others, but he was so poor he had no clothes that he could wear in which to be interviewed. At last he begged and borrowed, until he had enough money for his clothes and food, and set out for the castle.

He had almost come to the castle when he came upon a poor beggar at the side of the road. The beggar trembled, dressed only in rags. "Would you help me?" he cried weakly.

The young man was moved to compassion at the sight of the beggar and took off his new clothes and gave him his food. Then uncertain of what he should do, he slowly walked toward the castle. When he arrived, he was brought before the king and to his amazement, the king bowed before the young man.

Not wishing to offend the king, he hesitated. "You . . . you . . . were you the beggar by the road?"

"I was that beggar," said the king.

"But aren't you the king?"

"Yes, I am the king."

"I do not understand," stammered the young man in the beggar's rags.

"I had to find out if the one who followed me, who would be king, truly loved God and others. Only as a beggar with no claims on you but the love in your heart could I do that. Now I know you will rule my kingdom well."

Questions to Ponder: What did that story say to you? What would you have done if you had met the beggar on the road? How does the church help poor people?

If you use this story to introduce a stewardship project, have pictures of objects that will help the children see how their time and money and prayers can serve others, which is serving and loving God.

Reread the Bible verse, reminding the children that these are words Jesus said about people who help others.

124

When Jesus spoke of love, he told a story of the loving father who went against Semitic tradition to give his son his inheritance before the father was dead. It is a love too good to be true, but that is the love for which we all yearn.

God's power is the power of love. If we are the channels through which God's love flows into the world, we must be open to God, so that we can be fed, and open to the world, so that we may feed.

Love in a Lunchbox

And now faith, hope, and love abide, these three; and the greatest of these is love. (1 Cor. 13:13)

I can't find my homework!" "Why do I have to eat cereal?" "I hate school!" Each morning was filled with complaints and confusion. Getting children ready for school had to be the most difficult part of being a parent.

Mother was glad, therefore, that she had discovered how to pack love in a lunchbox.

Still grumbling, after he had reached school, the boy wondered why Mother was always so grouchy in the morning, forgetting that the morning had begun with Mother's pleasant voice and smiling face.

Then he remembered!

"You can't eat your lunch already!" said his friend. "School hasn't even started."

"I know," the boy replied, taking out his favorite sandwich and a small piece of white paper tucked inside the wrapper beside the sandwich. "WHEN YOU COME HOME WE WILL SHOP FOR THOSE SPECIAL SHOES I HAVE BEEN PROMISING YOU. I LOVE YOU, MOM," the boy read.

The boy smiled. Every morning in the kitchen, while the storm raged around her, Mother packed the boy's lunch and wrote him a small note, reminding him of her love.

The boy continued to smile as he saw the piece of his favorite chocolate cake. It was true—there was love in a lunchbox!

Questions to Ponder: Do you ever feel grouchy, as if there is a storm inside of you, as the boy in the story felt each morning before he went to school? How do you let people know that you love them?

Love is life's greatest gift and greatest challenge. Love is the way we value one another with our words and our actions. When a chair is broken, an ice cream cone dropped, a toe stubbed, love asks, "Are you all right?"

Huge Uncle Bill should have known better than to sit in that small chair; Caroline was told to pay attention to her ice cream; and Alex was asked to walk, not run. It was their fault that the accidents happened, but people are more important than things, where there is love.

Being loved, being valued, promotes self-confidence, learning, and growth. Love motivates. Love meets the needs of people. When our needs are met we have a sense of personal well-being and satisfaction. Love is an opportunity to give of oneself. Love is not an emotion. It is an attitude.

Love that is given out of the joy of giving will not think of reward or returned love. To say and show, "I love you for no reason at all, just because you are you" is a gift we can give others, because it is the gift we have been given by God. Such love supports, strengthens, and "graces" the life of the receiver. Such love makes one feel more alive, deeply significant and self-fulfilled. Such love provides creativity. It is a special kind of love.

Love One Another

"I give you a new commandment, that you love one another. Just as I have loved you, you also should love one another." (John 13:34)

T here was once a boy who felt that everyone was picking on him. When he awoke in the morning, his mother was grumpy. His sister argued with him all the time, and his father was mean to him. Wherever he was people seemed to be unhappy and grouchy. His teacher was pleasant to everyone but him, and he had few friends. "If I were stronger . . . or faster . . . or smarter . . . people would be kind to me," he thought.

One night as he sat pouting in the garden, an old woman appeared before him. "Who are you?" growled the boy.

"Who I am does not matter," the old woman replied. "Who are you?"

"I am the most picked on, unhappy person in the whole world," said the boy.

"Why are you so unhappy?" she asked.

"I am unhappy because people are mean to me."

The old woman looked at the boy kindly. "I have a secret that will change those people. It is written in the Bible."

The boy was interested. If only he could change the others, then he would be happy. "Will you sell it to me?"

126

The old woman shook her head no. "One does not sell secrets."

The boy was angry. "Then why did you bother to tell me about it!" he shouted. The boy stamped his foot and stood up and stalked away furiously.

The old woman spoke softly. "One does not sell secrets, but I will give it to you."

"Give it to me!" he exclaimed, excitedly.

The old woman handed a book to the boy. It looked as old as she did, for it had been used for many, many years. "The secret is in this book."

"I can't read yet," the boy said.

"Then I will whisper it in your ear," said the woman, bending over to tell him.

The next morning, when his mother awoke, she smiled at him. His sister spoke kindly to him. His father told him a joke he had heard. His teacher asked him to be leader of the day, and his friends invited him to play.

"God's law is a funny secret," the boy thought to himself. Someday he would share it with whoever wanted to change.

And the secret the old woman told the boy?

"Love one another."

Questions to Ponder: **Have you ever felt everyone was against you, that no one loved you? What was the secret the woman whispered in the boy's ear? Does it work?**

Seeing children as spiritual children of God, we can rejoice in their presence, and in their ability to hope and to love, while expressing our own love for them. Expressions of love are basic needs of all ages, words and deeds that clearly say, "I love you."

God is in the business of putting love into all creation and taking lives and transforming them. God's love teaches us to love. We can help children believe in a love that is being stored up for them, and trust that in this love there is strength and blessing.

Made in the image of God, who is love, we are coded to love, to be a loving presence in the world. For one human being to love another may be the most difficult of all our tasks and the work for which all other work is but preparation.

There is a story of a small boy watching a sculptor at work. For weeks the sculptor kept chipping away at a big block of marble. After a few weeks, he had created a beautiful marble lion. The little boy was amazed and said, "How did you know there was a lion in that rock?"

Love as a way of being is seeing the Christ in each person. Only the sculptor saw the lion in the rock. He saw with creative intelligence and spiritual awareness, something beyond sensory perception.

Rebecca

But be doers of the word, and not merely hearers who deceive themselves.
(James 1:22)

*R*ebecca is a symbol of unconditonal love in this church. Each member of this small but "mighty" church is an independent thinker and doer in his or her relationship with God.

Rebecca is also the daughter of the pastor. Adopted at birth, her new parents learned only much later that Rebecca was born deaf.

Although Rebecca may not be able to hear all of her father's words from the pulpit, even while sitting in the first row, she can hear coughing in the last pew and get up to remedy it with a cough drop.

You see, Rebecca is a participant rather than a spectator at church. One Sunday her mother was preaching at another church, so Rebecca joined the senior choir and sang with them. When it was time for the offering, Rebecca stood up and took the plate from the usher and passed it herself, and when her father left the altar, having pronounced the benediction, Rebecca joined him to process down the center aisle.

Rebecca is nine years old. She distributes the church bulletins, turns off the lights and heat after church worship service, and does whatever else needs to be done, for Rebecca is a "doer" of the word and not merely a "hearer."

Questions to Ponder: Have you ever known a "Rebecca" at church? Have you ever been a "Rebecca"? What would you do if you were Rebecca?

Children worship by imitating. They imitate the adults who kneel, fold their hands, close their eyes, and sing their hymns. They learn more from imitating than from listening. Religion is caught, not taught. We can lead children into worship but we cannot make them worship.

And sometimes a little child shall lead them.

One Sunday some of us gathered outside the church before the worship service. Enthusiastically engaged in conversation we were unaware that the service had begun, when a small voice said, "Is anyone coming to worship?" Without a word, we filed into the church behind, of course, Rebecca!

Rebecca reminds me of a woman on television who told about her child who has Down's syndrome: It's like planning a trip to Italy. You learn a bit of the language, study the books on geography and history and literature, you buy your ticket and pack your bag and board the plane. To your surprise you land in Holland and you are unprepared, but if you spend your time crying over not seeing Italy, you will miss the canals and windmills and the joy of the uniqueness of Holland. I would like to go to Italy but Italy is closed to me. I will enjoy Holland!

Showing Love

You shall love the LORD your God with all your heart, and with all your soul, and with all your might. (Deut. 6:5)

*T*he silver peso was José's most precious possession. Except for the clothes he wore, it was his only possession. Once it was not so, for he had owned many sheep, but José discounted sheep when there was gold to be had and with the other "hunters" he had gone off to the California hills to seek his fortune.

The day came, however, when there was but one coin in José's pocket, the silver one. "I will return to Mexico," he said, "but first I am hungry and tired. I will go to the church where there is food for me to eat and a place where I may sleep."

As he walked, a wicked plan began to form in José's mind. The church was known for its four beautiful, expensive silver candlesticks. They were very old and very expensive, and if they were stolen and sold, they would bring José a lot of money!

José needed money. Then and there he decided to steal the candlesticks and sell them in Mexico.

When José arrived at the church, the padre welcomed him, "Come in, my brother. Eat with us, for God is with the stranger."

José sat down and began to eat, but he sat apart from the others and did not speak. From where he sat he could see the church's altar and the four candlesticks with their candles burning brightly.

"I am tired," he mumbled to the priest, when he had eaten.

"Come with me, my brother. We have a place where you may sleep and rest as long as you have need."

As José walked to his room, he looked around to see how he would escape with the candlesticks. He smiled to himself, for it would be easy!

José put his candle on the table in his room. Something glistened brightly in its light. José leaned down to look more closely. There in the small basket were bright, shining coins, dozens of them!

"Someone has forgotten his money." José's eyes gleamed in the darkness. As he poured the coins into his pocket, they made so much noise, he put them back on the table. It was then that he noticed the small note in the bottom of the basket. José read the note aloud, "Let him who has greatest need take from the basket with God's blessing."

José read the words again before he understood what they meant. "They are here to be taken? Why, I could take one or all of the coins and no one would care. Food, lodging, money . . . and I do not have to do anything to earn it!"

José sat on the bed staring at the coins for a long time. Then he laughed. "I can take the coins and the candlesticks!"

José paced the floor. "My need is great! I have nothing but one peso to my name!" He could not get the coins out of his mind. "I will leave the candlesticks. It is wrong to steal from the church and I am young and strong and can work. I will take the money only."

José was tired. It was time to sleep. He lay on the bed, on his back, thinking. "I will only take part of the money in the basket."

But he could not sleep. "I did not take the candlesticks, for I am strong. I will work." He thought of the words in the basket, "Let him who has greatest need . . . greatest need . . . I am strong. Others will need the money more than I need it."

José jumped up and ran to his trousers. He took the silver peso from his pocket. "For those with greater needs," he said, dropping the peso in the basket.

Then José lay down and slept, and he slept well.

Questions to Ponder: **Why did José sleep well? To whom did he give his silver peso? (A silver peso is a Mexican coin worth about one dollar.) Have you ever been tempted to take something that does not belong to you? What is the "best" you have? What are some of the ways we can show love?**

A seven-year-old child packed her brother's and father's lunch. In a second bag she put hair ribbons, a few of her favorite stones, a toy doll, some raisins, pennies, a marble—all her special things. Her father, thinking it was junk, threw it away. When he came home that evening she asked, "Where is my bag?" "What bag?" "Oh, I forgot to put a note inside to tell you I was sharing my treasures with you, because I love you, Daddy," she said, hugging her father. He returned to his office quickly and retrieved the bag from the trash, for his daughter was saying, "Here, this is the best I have."

130

The Lion and the Mouse

Based on Luke 9:47-48.

A lion was sleeping in his lair, when a mouse, not knowing where he was going, ran over the mighty beast's nose and awakened him. The lion clapped his paw upon the frightened little creature, and was about to make an end of him, when the mouse, in pitiable tones, begged him to spare one who had not meant to offend. The lion, smiling at his little prisoner's fright, generously let him go. Now it happened not long after, that the lion, while hunting the woods for food, fell into the trap of the hunters, and finding himself entangled without hope of escape, set up a roar that filled the whole forest with its echo. The mouse, recognizing the voice of his friend, ran to the spot, and without more ado set to work to nibble the knot in the cord that bound the lion, and in a short time set the noble beast free; thus showing him that kindness is seldom thrown away, and that there is no creature so much below another but that he may have it in his power to return a good deed.

Questions to Ponder: What did this story say to you? Can being "little" be good?

Children can be a means of grace, when they express their caring concern. Being loved makes it possible to love oneself and then to love others.

An argument started among the disciples as to which one of them would be the greatest. Jesus, knowing their thoughts, took a little child and had him stand before him. Then he said to them, "Whoever welcomes this child in my name welcomes me, and whoever welcomes me welcomes the one who sent me; for the least among all of you is the greatest" (Luke 9:47).

In Luke 7:47 Jesus saw Mary Magdalene's great love, rather than her sins, for it is the characteristic of the true lover that the more one loves, the more one wants to love.

The power of the parable, the story, is that its metaphors make meaning, and because we hear stories on many different levels, each person for himself and herself, they are inexhaustible in their meaning. To explain a parable, however, means to fasten it with a given, permanent interpretation, thus preventing the possibility of the hearer to have personal insight, direction, or discovery.

Symbols and stories have power to reveal. They open up and disclose. They can point beyond themselves to a model or a truth they imitate or anticipate.

Love is an abstract, sacred symbol. God's love is revealed in the story of Jesus Christ's life, death, and resurrection, a love that "will not let us go."

Participating in Prayer

Adults can help children understand prayer as talking with God with trust rather than demand. Teaching a child to say "thank you" to God is more than using good manners. Prayer comes from the heart. The one who knows the Creator's love sings, for when our "cups" are full, they run over. When our hearts and minds are aware of God's glories and graces, praise is spontaneous.

Children need the inner resources that are provided in silence in the presence of God, in the faith imagination in which they feel the assurance of God's love and Jesus' presence, for prayer is the way children relate to God, and wonder is their worship. Children also need people who are excited by the "good news" of God's love in Jesus Christ.

Eight-year-old Heather, still wide-eyed with the excitement of seeing her first circus, came stumbling into the den, bursting to tell her mother of her adventure. She went on and on about the funny clowns, the beautiful ladies flying through the air, and the big elephants. She concluded her tale by declaring, "Oh Mama, it was so exciting that if you ever went to the circus you would never be satisfied with going to church again!" We have our work cut out for us!

Before I Sleep

I am still with you. (Ps. 139:18b)

Rabbits in their burrows,
Robins in their nest,
I and my blue blanket
Snuggle down to rest.
"I need a drink of water!"

133

"A light so I can see!"
"I need another kiss!"
"Please, just one more hug for me!"
"One more prayer and thank you,
God, Just one more peep
At the moon and stars above
Before I sleep!
Kittens with their mothers,
Does beside their deer,
The wonder of the nighttime is
Someone very near.
Thank you, dear God,
For being here."

Questions to Ponder: **Prayer is talking with God. We can talk with God anywhere and at any time, but special times are before eating and sleeping. When do you talk with God?**

Children say some memorized and some spontaneous prayers. They know that when they pray, they are talking to God.

Early prayers are short and the language is simple. "Thank you, God, for . . . Amen." The child learns to pray and worship by doing, alone and with others.

Prayer is listening with the heart. It takes children time to listen. Transition from busy activities to quiet reflection takes time, but with time and modeling, children will learn how to pray, for prayer is an act of love. It is living in the presence of God.

Children have a right to their religious heritage. The value of helping children know God through prayer was demonstrated after the Korean War when U.S. Army doctors looked into the high death rate among enemy-captured American soldiers between eighteen and twenty-two years of age. The study showed that thousands of these deaths occurred not because of hunger or disease but something new, what the GIs themselves named "give-up-itis." When faced with isolation, discouragement, and defeat, they did not have the faith or hope that would have sustained them. They did not feel life was worth living. On the other hand, many of those with a robust faith came out of prison physically and emotionally undaunted by the experience. Prayer is a way of hoping and coping.

Confession

Why do the nations conspire,
and the peoples plot in vain? (Ps. 2:1)

Molly and Holly
And Billy and me
Are fighting over
The swing in the tree,
Shoving and pushing,
And tugging with glee,
The fighting's soon over
And *we're* in the tree.
But what does it matter?
Tomorrow 'twill be
Billy and Holly
'Gainst Molly and me!

Questions to Ponder: Why do people argue and fight? What is God's plan? How do we know God's plan?

Or, if you prefer:

The heavens declare God's righteousness, for God is judge. (adapted from Ps. 50:6)

Sometimes I say an angry word
Or make another cry,
Or can't get rid of hurtful thoughts
No matter how I try.
Sometimes I have to have *my* way,
Or won't do what I ought,
And close my mind and heart and ears
To things that I've been taught.
I'd like to say "I'm sorry, God,"
And give my way all to you.
So please forgive me, God, and help
Me be more loving, too.

Pray together:

135

Dear God, we confess that we have done what we did not mean or want to do and have not done so many things we knew would be pleasing to you. Help us to understand and love one another. Amen.

Children, as Jesus' disciples, need to learn how to pray. Because young children do not admit their wrongdoing or see these actions as sins, confessions at this age are unreal. For preschool children, forgiveness comes from their parents. Therefore, meaningful prayers of confession are expressed later in the child's life. Prayers for forgiveness are only real when children are old enough to feel sorry and to recognize their responsibility for their actions and the consequences of those actions, although adults can interpret hurts to others.

In 1960 Ruby, a six-year-old, was one of four African-American children who participated in the desegregation of one of two New Orleans public schools. Though she was insulted and threatened, each night she prayed for those responsible "because Christ had told her that she must forgive these people because they didn't know what they were doing." Ruby knew exactly what she was doing because she had biblical sanction for her courageous suffering.

We do not know how God answers prayer but we believe that God uses our prayers, because Jesus prayed and taught us to pray, and because we have experienced for ourselves. Yet, as rational adults we sometimes ask, "Why teach children something they cannot understand or will have to outgrow later? I'll wait."

No parent, however, waits to teach their children the importance of good eating and health habits. There are "spiritual" habits as well.

God Listens to My Prayers

> *I love the* LORD, *because he hears me;*
> *he listens to my prayers.*
> *He listens to me*
> *every time I call to him. (Ps. 116:1-2 GNB)*

God doesn't talk with me. Why should I talk with God?" Molly asked her father. "If God won't talk with me, I won't talk with God!"
"Let me tell you a story, Molly . . . "
Nicodemus came to Jesus in the dark, questioning. "God doesn't speak to me."
"You must be born from above," Jesus replied.
"Huh?"

"The wind blows where it chooses. You hear the sound of it (you may even feel it) but you do not see it or know from where it comes or where it goes. So it is with everyone who is born of the Spirit."

"That's an explanation?"

"Oh, you want an explanation. Nicodemus, you have come to the wrong person. I will tell you a story."

Her father turned to Molly. *"Read* A Wrinkle in Time, *Molly. Mrs. Whatsit is a very wise woman. She may even be an angel."*

Then he laughed. *"No, Molly, I won't explain to you 'angels.'"*

So Molly found A Wrinkle in Time *and read aloud, "Explanations are not easy when they are about things for which your civilization still has no words."*

Questions to Ponder: Do you think things always have an explanation? Does God speak to you? How does God speak?

God is the source of life and love, of intelligence and imagination. Through prayer we become aware that God is at work in the world, but God's ways are not our ways and God's time is not our time. One of the ways God works in the world is through prayer. Through God's empowering through prayer, we can smash the limits of fear and doubt. As atoms are smashed to release great physical power, so prayer sets free our spiritual power.

Hearing words does not mean children understand the meaning of the words. Speak slowly, simply, and distinctly when you pray. Praying to God does not mean things will work out the way we want. Pray as if you expect to learn something and wait for a response, be it an idea or feeling. God's love works through us.

I believe God speaks through the scriptures, through prayer, people, and the events of our lives. Perhaps we do not hear God because we have learned to confine God's way of speaking. Perhaps we do not hear God because we have put God so high and far away? Perhaps God is as near as the air we breathe. Perhaps God is in our breathing, in the thoughts we think, and the feelings we feel.

God is always this and that and more than this and that and other than this and that. The book of Job allows God to be God. God does not answer Job's complaints. God finally speaks, saying, "Job, look at creation!"

All of us have questions and doubts and seek answers and explanations. Madeleine L'Engle wrote the book, *A Wrinkle in Time*, as an example of the willing suspension of disbelief, which Mrs. Murry, Meg's mother, a scientist, is willing to do. When Meg, the heroine of the story, asks, "Do you think things always have an explanation?" her mother replied, "Yes. I believe that they do. But I think that with our human limitations we're not always able to understand the explanations. But you see, Meg, just because we don't understand doesn't mean that the explanation doesn't exist. . . . I don't understand it any more than you do, but one thing I've learned is that you don't have to understand things for them to be."[1] God finally gave up on the Word being heard or understood, and the Word became flesh to dwell among us, the Word became visible, was seen and heard.

Children build their learning on "concrete" trust. How can we trust God whom we cannot see or touch? Children learn trust from the people around them: parents, teachers, friends, and family members. What we do speaks louder than what we say. Perhaps Molly's father was able to say, "When I am trustworthy, God speaks through me, but I am human and make mistakes, so God gave us a map for our guidance. We call that map that tells us God cares the 'Bible.' God also gave us God's Spirit within us to guide us, and the sacred story of Jesus, whom we call Lord."

Finally, words halt behind intuition and imagination. We sense there is a Creator because we can see and touch, hear and smell, and taste creation. And sometimes, in prayer, be it alone, in community, in sanctuary, or woods, we feel God's nearness.

In the Beginning

Then the LORD God formed man from the dust of the ground, and breathed into his nostrils the breath of life; and the man became a living being. (Gen. 2:7)

In the beginning
There was only you,
God, weren't you lonely
With nothing to do?
Is that why you made
The creatures and me?
Do even Creators
Need company?
God, we are grateful
That you are everywhere,
Fathering and mothering the heaven
And earth with your care.

Questions to Ponder: **Why do you think God created the world? For what are you most glad? Close your eyes and try to imagine before creation when all was dark and without form. What do you see? Do you think God could be lonely? Jesus called God "Father," another name for God. When you pray, what name do you give God? Many people think of God as a "mother," as well as a "father."**

Prayer is the way children relate to God, and wonder is their worship. Wonder can lead to a meaningful relationship with a loving God, and this relationship can be the most important factor in the child's life, for when the child feels God's unconditional love, he or she has the security and trust, the peace that passes all understanding, and the strength needed to become what God intends the child to become.

For many years I lived next door to Sarah. I was there when she was born. I rocked her to sleep, telling her stories and singing her songs, night after night. And because Sarah's grandmother lived in Florida, and I lived next door, Sarah, as she grew, called me her "fake" grandmother.

The other day Sarah, who is now twelve, asked her mother, "Do I have to believe in God?"

Her mother calmly replied, "It is mighty lonely if you don't."

Faith is a mutual relationship with God and life is bigger than we are or our views of it are. As Sarah's mother said, "It is lonely without God." There are times when we cannot do it alone. More than that, like it or not, we are dependent.

Yet we forget. The demands, the world's values, rob us of time and trust. Jesus, as the Parable of God, came to minister to those in need, for he knew their need for wholeness, health, and harmony. God is with us, as we pray. God created us for relationship and prayer.

By listening to children's feelings over disappointments, quarrels, longings and sorrows, guilts and griefs, and what they see on television, a person realizes that the "talkings from the heart" is prayer.

Praying at Night

For darkness is as light to you. (Ps. 139:12c)

Now it's time for me to sleep,
I pray, dear God, that you will keep
Me safe within Your love this night
And wake me with the morning's light. Amen.

Night
spreads a blanket on the bed
and tucks in earth from foot to head.
The stars,
are friendly lamps of light,
so earth won't be afraid at night.

Questions to Ponder: **What are the words you pray at night? Why did God plan for stars?**

Read the Bible verse aloud from your Bible.

Poems can be used as prayers and as a way to introduce talking together about the child's thoughts and feelings in relation to God.

Children can understand metaphors that are related to their experiences and readily relate to imaginative images. The poem will help children to view God's world of nature as friendly and personal.

Short, quiet poems can set an atmosphere for sleep, transforming the hectic, busy activities of day into the slow, restful routines of night.

Sometimes fear is stronger than faith. In the dark children fear "monsters."

"Why are you afraid? God is here!"

"Please send God away and put on the light."

Your presence, or someone "big" the child trusts, is the light.

Praise the Lord

Praise the LORD! (Ps. 106:1)

The heavens are glad,
The skies are full,
And every floating cloud
And flying bird sings aloud
To praise the Lord.

The earth rejoices,
The land gives birth,
And every bursting seed

And blooming flower sings indeed
To praise the Lord.

The sea roars,
The waters leap,
And every sandy shore
And swimming fish joyfully adore
And praise the Lord.

The fields exult,
The lambs grow fat,
And every creeping thing
And growing grain begins to sing
To praise the Lord.

The trees blossom,
Sing for joy,
And every bud
And greening leaf
Sing songs that flood
To praise the Lord. (Based on Psalm 96:11-12.)

Questions to Ponder: **For what do you give God praise?**

Sing a familiar song the children know, praising God.

Children imitate adults. Before meals and bedtime and during pauses throughout the day offer opportunities for prayers of praise and thanksgiving.

When adults sing or say with eyes and heart open, "Thank you, God, for Karen's kindness" or "Thank you, God, for the wonderful rain," "Thank you, God, for Lauren's gift of drawing . . . for this macaroni and cheese we are about to eat . . . your plan for us to grow . . . for Jesus . . . for mothers and fathers who love us," it shows an attitude of wonder and awe.

The sound of a bird, the first flower of spring or snow of winter, a sunset, the dew on the grass, and the moon and the stars, are all opportunities for expressing praise and thanksgiving.

10·18·94

Praying

"Hear my prayer, O LORD." (Ps. 39:12a)

God doesn't like me," Brad said to his teacher.

"Why do you say that?" she asked.

"I prayed for a sunny day yesterday and it rained and we couldn't go to the zoo as planned."

Kathy had been listening and could be silent no longer. "But you have to take your turn, Brad. Someone else prayed for a rainy day!"

Questions to Ponder: Have you ever prayed for something that did not happen as you wanted, as Brad did? Do you agree with Kathy?

Center in silence with the children. Centering is the way we become quiet and invite God into our minds to listen and speak with us. Find a quiet, comfortable place (your worship center), where you can sit. Place your feet on the floor, your hands in your lap. Close your eyes and take three slow, deep breaths. Feel the closeness of God. Let Jesus take your hand or sit on Jesus' lap as the children did long ago. Feel Jesus hug you. Hear with your "inner" ears. Let go of your thoughts. Be open to whatever comes to you, and use your imagination, for that is the way God speaks to you.

Quietness comes from inside. Imagine you are "floating on a cloud," or "center" yourself by thinking of water—a lake, an ocean, a beach. Let the water soothe you for as long as you like.

It is more important to teach children to pray than to teach prayers. Memorized prayers can become routine, as the child reminds us, "I know my prayer so well I can say it without thinking."

Young children think of God as the Great Magician because they are "magical" thinkers. Thinking of God as the Great Parent, they expect God to give them what they want.

A young boy wanted a bicycle and his grandmother said, "If you want a bicycle, you need to sit down and write Jesus a letter." So the boy wrote, "Dear Jesus, if you will send me a bicycle, I will be good for a whole year." The more he thought about how long a year was, the more he wondered, and at last he tore up the letter and began again. "Dear Jesus," he wrote, "if you will send me a bicycle, I will be good for a whole month." But even a month seemed long, as he thought about it. Again he tore up the letter and wrote, "Dear Jesus, if you will send me a bicycle, I will be good for this entire week."

142

Even a week, however, could be an eternity and so he went to the mantle and took down the statue of the Mother Mary, wrapped her in a towel, and put her in the closet. Then he sat down and wrote, "Dear Jesus, if you ever want to see your mother again . . . "

Adults, however, can help children to understand prayer as talking with God with trust rather than demand.

Praying with Wonder

My mouth is filled with your praise,
and with your glory all day long. (Ps. 71:8)

> Dear God,
> I cannot wrap a mountain up
> Or give the Sea away.
> I cannot make the Robin sing
> Or buy a sunny Day.
> I cannot cause a Flower to bloom
> Or catch the Wind at play.
> I cannot paint a Sunset,
> But I can pause and pray.
> Thank you, Lord, for the majesty
> And mystery of your creation
> Within and without. Amen.

Questions to Ponder: **What are some of the things God has made? What does the poem say we can do?**

Or

Ask the children to illustrate the following poem of praise:
(Each line is to be read by a different person.)

> Praise God, sun and moon,
> praise God, all you shining stars.
> Praise God, you highest heavens.
> Praise the Lord from the earth,
> you sea creatures and all ocean depths,
> lightning and hail, snow and clouds,
> stormy winds that do his bidding,

you mountains and all hills,
fruit trees and all cedars,

wild animals and all cattle,
small creatures and flying birds,
kings of the earth and all nations, Praise the Lord!

Charles was five the summer we vacationed at Padre Island. Arising early one morning, I saw the sun make its magnificent appearance, covering the ocean in a brilliant, shimmering red. I called, "Charles, wake up. Come see the sun rise!"

A sleepy boy rubbed his eyes, following my invitation, but taking one look at the sun, he ran from the room to return to his bedroom. "Charles," I cried, "what is the matter?"

Charles appeared suddenly from his room, out of his pajamas and fully dressed, saying, "I had to dress for the sun."

To see with the heart invites us to see the "extra" in the ordinary, the sacredness of everyday things, the presence of God among us here and now, and the interrelationship with all creation. The source of wonder, the ability to appreciate the concrete, particular, unique gifts of creation, is the imagination. Poetry and parable invite imagination to participate, to step inside and live its truth from within. "Perhaps this is how it happened, how he felt, what she thought," and in the "perhaps" we experience truth at a deeper level than logic, for symbolic expressions are experienced in this way, making us truly human and fully alive.

Thanksgiving Day

Praise the LORD!
I will give thanks to the LORD with my whole heart,
in the company of the upright, in the congregation. (Ps. 111:1)

Thanksgiving Day the church bells ring,
The congregation comes to sing
Of purple mountain majesties.
At church, at home, in families
We sing our praise to God for love,
For faith and food and sun above,
For everything that God provides,
The stars, the rain, the sea, the skies.

144

Questions to Ponder: **For what would you like to thank God?**

(Pray together, asking each child to add one sentence of thanksgiving.)

We learn to pray by praying, just as we learn to love by loving. Who knows? Perhaps someday we may even get it "right." Until then we have God's promise to be with us and Christ's sacrifice of love.

The child's world goes beyond the home. My granddaughter does not attend church, but she does attend a preschool in a church. At Thanksgiving her father prepared a magnificent meal. It did not seem proper for us to eat it without a blessing, but he is not in the habit of meal praying. Before I had a chance to suggest it, Lauren said, "But what about the blessing, Daddy? Aren't we going to pray?" A little child can lead us.

The Lord's Prayer

He said to them, "When you pray, say . . . " (Luke 11:2)

*O*ne *day Jesus sat in the garden with a friend. The air was still. The garden was quiet. Neither of the two men spoke.*

Suddenly Jesus closed his eyes. His friend became sad because he knew that Jesus was far away from him. He knew, too, that when Jesus closed his eyes, he received a special power, and his friend wanted that power. He wanted that power more than anything else in the world.

Jesus' friend was big. He was strong. Why, he could wrestle anyone and would always win. He was stronger than Jesus, but Jesus had a special power. It was almost as if Jesus knew a secret. If only he could know that secret that gave his friend such power and strength and courage! He would give anything to know that secret.

Yet, as much as he wanted to know Jesus' secret, he had never asked him. The man thought to himself, "He would refuse me. He would say 'No.' He would laugh at me." The man was afraid to ask.

Because he was afraid, he never asked Jesus to tell him the secret of his power. The more he thought about it now, the more he wanted to know the secret. Oh, he would give anything to know!

When Jesus opened his eyes, the man looked into them. They were kind and thoughtful. The man wondered why he had been afraid. His friend would not laugh at him. His friend would not refuse him. His friend loved him. But did he love him enough to give away the secret of his power? The man shook his head, sadly.

145

Again he looked into the eyes of Jesus. This friend loved him. That was part of his power. At last he arose and looked down at his friend. He stuttered the words as he spoke. "I . . . I . . . would . . . could . . . you . . . " He stopped. Then quickly, all in one breath and with all the courage he could manage, he said, "I would like to know the secret of your power."

Jesus looked up at him and smiled. Then he, too, stood up, and with a gentle but firm voice, replied, "When you pray, say, 'Our Father who is in heaven, blessed be your name. Your rule come, your will be done, on earth as it is in heaven. Give us today our daily bread. Forgive us our sins, as we forgive those who do us wrong. And lead us not into temptation, but deliver us from evil.' "

Jesus gazed deeply into his friend's eyes. "Being with my Father in prayer— that is my secret."[2]

Questions to Ponder: **Why do we pray? What good are our prayers? Why did Jesus say, "Our Father"?**

Jesus said, "Our Father," a symbolic way of saying God is like a parent, whether father or mother, someone greater who guides and nourishes us. God as Parent evokes an attitude and experience of the mystery of our being loved.

All life is relational. In a relationship we want to know one another. Faith is our relationship with God. Prayer is the way we communicate. Use "God" in place of "he" unless it becomes awkward. Words matter, but children fill words with their experiences. How you act gives words their meaning.

Many children possess a special sense of the world, for children experience before they know and know before they conceptualize. Through imagination and religious experience the Holy Spirit enables us to be open to the inner power that awakens us to the presence of God. When properly understood, the imagination can reveal the deeper aspects of truth and reality. It supports and strengthens faith. An attentive imagination reveals and celebrates the mystery of creation, for it is the fundamental capacity to open us to the world of spirit.

The Ring

O LORD, make haste to help me. (Ps. 40:13b)

Mother asks, "Carol, have you seen my ring?"
Lovely, sparkling, moonlit thing
rules my finger like a queen.

Castles, princes, islands
seem suddenly to appear,
ancient fairy tales come near.
See it shimmer! See it glow!
All I need to say is "No . . . "
I could hide it in a place where she would never see,
I could keep it . . . ,
'Twould be mine . . .
O, Lord, please make haste to help me!

Questions to Ponder: **To whom does the ring on Carol's finger belong? Why does Carol want to keep it? How can God help Carol?**

Prayer is talking and listening with God. Sometimes it is simply sitting with God without thoughts or words, just as you sometimes sit with your best friend, enjoying his or her love and company. Being with God is more than saying to God what you feel and think, although that is important. It can also include closing your eyes and letting go of thinking. This kind of prayer helps us be near Jesus who otherwise might seem faraway and long ago. In prayer, stories about Jesus are here and now. We can enter the story through our faith imagination and see Jesus look at us, hear Jesus speak to us, and respond to Jesus in love.

Because prayer is a relationship with God, children can be encouraged to use their own thoughts and feelings in talking with God. We have taught children to speak to God who loves them. Have we taught them to listen? There are five kinds of prayer: *praise, thanksgiving, confession, intercession,* and *petition.* Young children pray prayers for help and thanksgiving. Avoid petitionary prayers that are like asking God to be "Santa Claus." When these prayers, such as petition and intercession ("Make Grandma well.") are not answered, children want to know "Why doesn't God answer my prayer?" or think "God doesn't like me," or "God is mean."

Children pray prayers of petition and there are many citations for such from scripture: "Ask, and it will be given you . . . ," the woman who nagged the judge and Jesus told us to pray as that woman, "When you pray, say, 'Give us this day our daily bread.' "

If we don't know how to ask for the little things, how will we know how to ask for the great?

On the other hand prayer is neither "pretty please" nor "Aladdin's lamp." Prayer is not manipulating God, but prayer releases an energy that if not for the prayer would be blocked. We are collaborators with

147

God. In some way God uses our prayers. Prayer is both "Thy will be done" and "Papa, Mama, we need . . . "

Word Watch

Set a guard over my mouth, O LORD;
keep watch over the door of my lips. (Ps. 141:3)

Dear Lord, when my friend Fred tells me about
The fish he caught last week,
Small, swaggering soldiers stream outside
My lips with swords to speak.
And when my friend Nancy laughs about
The dress her neighbor wears,
They change to swarms of buzzing bees
That bite and sting in pairs.
And some will tease and some will hurt,
And some are simply slips.
O Lord, please put a guard to watch
The doorway of my lips. Amen.

Questions to Ponder: **What do the "small, swaggering soldiers with swords" represent? What are the "buzzing bees that bite and sting"? What "teases" and "hurts" in the poem? What would be a good name for the poem?**

Words are important to children. Words are symbols of the world we carry in our heads. They represent, stand for, realities of things, events, visions, and feelings. For children they are magic incantations. When they say "milk," they are rewarded magically by the gift of the pure, white liquid.

Words stand for love, justice, forgiveness, and God, creating images in the mind. When Carl Jung described himself as a "splinter of the infinite deity," I understood his words: "We are born that we might become, as a conscious individual, a new life form of God."

Before children understand abstract, theological, or biblical words, they hear and respond to the love and assurance of the people who use them. We, therefore, not only use the words of faith but translate these words into living experiences. Give no words when action is possible. What children can do for themselves, let them do. The important thing

148

is not so much that every child should be taught as that every child should be given the desire and opportunity to learn.

Children are concrete thinkers. Returning from his first day at school, our six-year-old son described saying the pledge of allegiance: "We put our eating hand over our heart and said our prayers to the flag."

And children are imaginative. They grow into and out of prayer, for prayer for children is an attitude of openness to God and to wonder in God's creation.

Experiencing Wonder

There is potential holiness in the uncommon commonplace, if we allow wonder its proper place in our perception of the world.

Wonder is one of the two faculties by which we look at the world. Reason is the other. Reason is the compass that directs us to the pole of meaning.

The little prince said, "The men where you live raise five thousand roses in the same garden—and they do not find in it what they are looking for."

"They do not find it?" I replied.

"And yet what they are looking for could be found in one single rose, or in a little water."

"Yes, that is true," I said.

And the little prince added: "But the eyes are blind. One must look with the heart."[1]

To see with the heart, the imagination, invites us to see the "extra" in the ordinary, the sacredness of everyday things, the presence of God among us here and now. It is imagination that can bind the brokenness between matter and spirit, the bridge between the wholeness of creation and the divine.

God implanted wonder within every child.

A Quiet Walk

And after he had dismissed the crowds, he went up the mountain by himself to pray. When evening came, he was there alone. (Matt. 14:23)

Shhh! I'm taking a quiet walk.
I'm strolling inside my mind.
Don't anyone talk.
I need to be alone
To see if I can find
A picture or a poem,
A feeling that is all my own,
So please don't talk,
For I am taking a quiet walk.

Questions to Ponder: **Do you ever take a "quiet walk"? Where do you go? What do you do, see, hear, wonder?**

To wonder is to see with the heart. To wonder is to appreciate and be "at home" with mystery and silence. Mystery is an integral part of creation, of every person. To be in tune with mystery is to seek and find an inner harmony that lends strength and meaning to all of life. It is to find God. To wonder at God's creation is to see God in all.

Children need the inner resources that are provided in silence in the presence of God, in the faith imagination in which they feel the assurance of God's love, for prayer is the way children relate to God and wonder is their worship.

Silence is a part of wonder. It seems as if today we are afraid of silence, afraid to be alone, afraid to be with God, yet it is in the silence that we take time to experience the presence of God. "Hurried" children need time to withdraw to pretend and imagine. They need silence to experience awe and wonder in the world within and the world outside. They need silence to be creative to discover new possibilities, and to cope with the complexities and confusions of their busy, perplexing world.

All the Earth

The earth is the LORD's and the fullness thereof,
the world and those who dwell therein. (Ps. 24:1 RSV)

"All of the earth belongs to me,
heaven and harbor,
sand and sea,
tiger and turtle,
sun and seed,
daylight and darkness, word and deed."

All of creation is the Lord's,
made by God's plan.
And in God's happiness
shared with woman and man.

Questions to Ponder: **Where do you have a sense of being with God, or encountering God? When do you feel God's love?**

Edward Robinson in *The Original Vision,* reports on the religious experience of childhood. Through his interviews with some 360 or so men and women fifty years old and older, asking them to write of "any way that their lives had been affected by some power beyond themselves," he found that children as young as four and five, with their natural capacity of imagination, understanding, and knowing, have experiences that are essentially religious, but which only in later life they can name, describe, and explain. The religious imagination, religious feeling, the sense of the sacred, is experienced before it is expressed.

Many interviewees repeatedly expressed a sense of deep and overwhelming gratitude for the beauty of nature: the calm, misty mornings; the dew on the grass, sparkling as iridescent jewels in the sunlight; and the almost friendly protection of surrounding trees. It was a sense of unending peace and security, of love and living presence of all that they had ever loved, and yet it was something much more.

Over and over persons expressed that they knew these things because they had experienced a "constant force at work from the inside," moments of pure joy that "served as an inescapable sense of assurance" and "the certainty of ultimate good" for which "[they felt] the profoundest gratitude."

Children have a strong sense of wonder. They approach the mysterious, the unknown, with imagination, exploration, and freedom of expression. When the imagination is stimulated from a store of information and stories, children are encouraged to express their own feelings and thoughts in a variety of ways; but wonder, mystery, creativity can be lost when imagination, exploration, and freedom of expression are limited.

Water

[The LORD] prepares rain for the earth. (Ps. 147:8b)

*I*t has been a cold week, hasn't it?" the teacher asked. "As I walked past my plants in the garage, without sunlight, they looked sad to me. I look forward to *the day they can leave the dark garage and come out into the sunlight, for what do·plants need?"*

"Sun." "Water," the children replied.

"Yes, plants need water and sun. How much water? Can plants get too much water? What would happen if they got too much water?"

"They would drown and die."

"Jesus told stories about seeds and plants and growing. They were metaphors. What is a metaphor?" she asked.

"Something that means something else," Jason replied.

"Yes, Jesus' stories were about God and the kingdom of God. As I looked at the sad plants without water and sunlight, I thought of people in 'garages.' What do people need?"

The children were silent. They were thinking. Then they spoke: "Help." "Encouragement." "Love."

The teacher smiled in agreement. "How do we show love?"

"Smile." "Share our toys." "Pray."

Then the teacher used a metaphor. "Can we pour too much love on people, as water on plants? Can we overdo love? We sprinkle the plants with water and the people with love."

The teacher took from her bag several small baskets, as she said, "I have a small basket for each of you filled with imaginary water to sprinkle on one another and on the congregation." (Distribute tiny baskets.)

The pastor, seated among the children, also received a tiny basket and upon entering the pulpit, sprinkled the people with love.

Play a recording of water sounds. If possible project on-screen a slide of a waterfall, running brook, ocean, a glass of water, or use a video featuring water movement. If you are using a recording of water sounds or slides or video, play the sounds as the children gather, before telling the story.

Questions to Ponder: **Beside an empty glass and a pitcher of water on the altar, share stories of places where people have nothing to drink. Pour the water into the glass. Use a microphone to magnify the sound of water, explaining how we can make a difference by digging new wells and pipelines provided by the money we share, and our prayers for water. What did the story say to you? Whom do you "sprinkle" with love? Who "sprinkles" you?**

Children need opportunities to share their love and wonder, their gifts of money, talents, and time. Give them opportunities to understand God's love for all people and Jesus' command to "love one another," which includes the world in which we live (plants and animals and people).

The Lilies

"Consider the lilies, how they grow: they neither toil nor spin; yet I tell you, even Solomon in all his glory was not clothed like one of these. But if God so clothes the grass of the field, which is alive today and tomorrow is thrown into the oven, how much more will he clothe you." (Luke 12:27-28)

> *The lilies are growing*
> *In petals of white,*
> *Their beauty is showing*
> *And giving delight.*
> *If God loves the flowers*
> *And planned what they wore,*
> *God must love God's children*
> *So much more!*

Questions to Ponder: Jesus said in the Bible that God loves us so much we need not worry. How do you know God loves you?

Children have a keen sense of the awareness of beauty and wonder. They see "unwrapped gifts and free surprises," the world "fairly studded and strewn with pennies cast broadside from a generous hand." Annie Dillard in *Pilgrim at Tinker Creek* reminds me that I want to see as children see. Children keep their eyes open, for they are still uncluttered by material things. Dillard told of how all of her adult life she had wished to see the cemented case of a caddisfly larva. One day as she sat on the bank side by side with Sally Moore, the young daughter of friends, the young girl found one on the pebbled bottom of the shallow stream. "What's this?" she asked. Annie wrote, "That, I wanted to say as I recognized the prize she held, is a memento mori for people who read too much."[2]

Many of today's adults are aware of the developmental theories of when a child is ready to do this or that and are comfortable with prediction. But possibility, grace, and the flame of the inward light, are less known or understood. Yet adults recalling their early childhood experiences remember the sense of closeness with the one whom we call God.

The Wonder of the Seed and of the Story

In the beginning . . . God said, "Let the earth put forth vegetation: plants yielding seed." (Gen. 1:1, 11)

A Sower went out to sow his seed.
"Hey!"
The Sower looked around to see.
There was no one there.
"Hey, Sower!"
The Sower looked again and saw no one. "Where are you? Who are you?"
"You ought to know me. I am one of your seeds."
The Sower opened his sack.
"Hi!" said the Seed. "What are you doing?"
"I am about to plant you," explained the Sower.
"That's good. I want to grow, but . . . "
"Yes?"
"May I choose where I live?"
"Well . . . all right. Come along."
The Sower and the Seed walked on the way.
"How about here where the birds live?" the Sower asked. "You could hear their music every morning and evening."
"It's a possibility," agreed the Seed. "What else is there to choose?"
The Sower and the Seed walked on the way until they came to rocky ground.
"Would you like to live among the rocks? You could see the mountains shimmering in the sunlight, for here the sun shines brightly."
"It's a possibility," agreed the Seed. "What else is there to choose?"
The Sower and the Seed walked on the way until they came to a beautiful rosebush.
"Would you like to live with the rosebush? You could smell the perfume of the roses," said the Sower.
"It's a possibility," agreed the Seed. "What else is there to choose?"
The Sower and the Seed walked on the way until they came to an old hut by the side of the road where an old man and woman lived. They were poor but

155

happy. Around the hut the woman had planted a garden of green peas and beans, and yellow daffodils and purple pansies in the good ground.

"Would you like to live among the poor? You could grow here and share what you have," said the Sower.

"It's a possibility," said the Seed.

The Seed looked back down the way to the rosebush, the mountains shimmering in the sun, and the path where the birds lived.

It was time to choose.

"I don't know," said the Seed.

It was not easy to choose.

The Sower sat down beside the Seed. "Let me tell you a story," he said.

"Listen! A sower went out to sow. And as he sowed, some seed fell on the path, and the birds came and ate it up. Other seed fell on rocky ground, where it did not have much soil, and it sprang up quickly, since it had no depth of soil. And when the sun rose, it was scorched; and since it had no root, it withered away. Other seed fell among thorns, and the thorns grew up and choked it, and it yielded no grain. Other seed fell into good soil and brought forth grain, growing up and increasing and yielding thirty and sixty and a hundredfold" (Mark 4:3-8).

The seed, nestled in the lap of the Sower, stood up and smiled, waving good-bye as it walked toward the small hut and the good ground where he grew and lived happily ever after, thanks to the Sower and the story. . . .

Questions to Ponder: **Have seeds for the children to see and touch and wonder with. Close with a prayer for the wonder of seeds that grow in the ground and are watered and warmed by God's rain and sun, and for stories that grow "inside" of people, "watered" and "warmed" by hearing and telling them over and over.**

You might prefer to use the story as a skit with a sower and a seed.

Wonder is the way children worship. Children become aware of God through wonder, which is their way of worship. Wonder can lead to a meaningful relationship with a loving God, and this relationship can be the most important factor in the child's life, for when the child feels God's unconditional love, he or she has the security and trust, the peace that passes all understanding, and the strength needed to become what God intends the child to become.

When we reach children, as we sometimes do, it is generally on a point of sheer delight so natural to them, for a child's natural attitude is wonder. To the child, everything is new. Children's vision is clearer because they have fewer preconceptions. They keep their eyes and hearts open to wonder.

Symbols and religious imagination have an important place in Christian formation. The religious language of story, parable, poetry, metaphor, and symbol describe an alternative world to the one in which we live in a technological society.

I Have a Place

The LORD takes pleasure . . . in those who hope in his steadfast love.
(Ps. 147:11)

> I have a place that's all my own,
> That's hidden, secret, and alone,
> Where nobody goes, and nobody knows,
> But me.
> A secret spot might be a tree,
> A closet door closed quietly,
> A place in your mind that no one can find
> Or see,
> A growing garden, woods, or stream,
> Some silent place to think, and pray,
> And dream.

Questions to Ponder: **Where do you think, and dream, and pray?**

To encounter God in wonder and mystery, sacred time and space, in the imagination, the quiet place within, can communicate a sense of holiness. The question is how do we talk or write about it.

Children choose to interpret life with meaning without thinking or debating about it. They grow up in a relationship with the Being who balances their world and through whom they interpret or understand that world.

They experience, until we teach them otherwise, their importance to that One, the value of their existence, the sense that there is no one else like themselves, no one else who could take their place.

Every person needs a garden, a corner, a place in the mind set aside for rest, enjoyment, and imagination, a place to dream, for imagination is a source of pleasure, of mastery, of coping, and of creative activity. Imagination is the bringing of the new into being!

I have a place where I can be alone.
It's cool and bare,
And quiet there
And all my very own.
The only company I have is space.
But God is there,
God's everywhere,
The world's God's dwelling place.

Fantasy helps fill huge gaps in the child's understanding, which are due to inner pressures, immaturity, and lack of information. The child becomes comfortable with his "unconscious" by spinning out day-dreams and fantasizing, thus developing his inner resources, so that the emotions, intellect, and imagination support and enrich one another.

Wonder and the gift of fantasy feed and preserve the imagination. Albert Einstein felt that the gift of fantasy meant more to him than his talents for absorbing positive knowledge.

An exercised imagination produces faith and reveals deeper aspects of spiritual reality. It is the fundamental capacity for insight that is the source of all knowledge and love and meaning.

Listening

*Let everything that breathes praise the LORD!
Praise the LORD!" (Ps. 150:6)*

I thought I heard the heavens speak.
I listened carefully,
And from afar the stars proclaimed
God's power and majesty.
I sang my praise to God who made
The sea, the earth, the sky.
Imagine my surprise to hear
The firmament reply!
In Sunday-dress the lilies prayed,
The trees bowed down their limbs,
While caroling birds in chorus praised
God's handiwork with hymns.

Questions to Ponder: **How do you hear "the heavens speak"? What other pictures did you see in your mind?**

One respondent in the book, *The Original Vision*, wrote, "When I was about five I had the experience on which, in a sense, my life has been based. . . . Every single person was a part of a Body, . . . This inner knowledge was exciting and absorbingly interesting, but it remained unsaid because, even if I could have expressed it, no one would have understood. Once, when I tried, I was told I was morbid."[3]

Another respondent recalled walking on the moors between the age of four and five: "In that moment I knew that I had my own special place, as had all other things, animate and so-called inanimate, and that we were all part of this universal tissue which was both fragile yet immensely strong, and utterly good and beneficient.

"The vision has never left me. It is as clear today as fifty years ago, and with it the same intense feeling of love of the world and the certainty of ultimate good. . . . The whole of this experience has ever since formed a kind of reservoir of strength from an unseen source."[4]

Over and over these people reported that they experienced, or were aware of, a Divine Presence, but were afraid to mention it because the adults in their lives were so unaware. There is more wisdom and awareness in many a child than in many adults; it is the adults who lose the simplicity of childhood and don't bother to find it again that make life complex for adolescents.

Tasting

O taste and see that the LORD is good. (Ps. 34:8a)

> I like to touch my tongue upon
> An ice-cream cone to lick,
> Or suck a soda through a straw,
> Or chew a licorice stick,
> Or bite into a hamburger,
> Or taste a chocolate treat,
> Or nibble on a nut, or eat
> Whatever's good and sweet.

Questions to Ponder: **What is your favorite food?**

Show me your favorite food without words while we guess what it is. (Take turns "showing" and guessing. Have a small food treat to taste, such as a colorful candy or a piece of apple.)

159

The child's way of knowing is intuitive, thinking-feeling, stirring the imagination to dream. Children learn through wonder and wonder through their senses. For children, the world is fresh and new and surprising. Children want to touch and taste, smell and see, hear and tell all that they can. They need opportunities to wade in puddles and walk in the rain, to dig in the dirt and stare at sunsets, to stay up late and hear the sounds of the dark, or get up early and observe the beginnings of day. Children should be encouraged to chase butterflies and discover doodlebugs and sticky slugs, to hug trees, and to laugh at the sky. Children find meaning in every bush and rock and tree, because children are still safe in the "sacred groves," close to God. Wonder is a way of looking at life in silence, alone or together, on mental tiptoes.

The Dew

Praise [God], sun and moon;
  praise [God], all you shining stars! (Ps. 148:3)

Tomorrow morning
In the dawn,
The only jewels
Left on the lawn
Will shine one moment in the sun,
And then be gone.

Questions to Ponder: **What is the most beautiful thing you have ever seen? Have you ever seen the dew on the grass the first thing in the morning, before the sun rises? Name the "shining" things you know.**

(Have a "jewel" to show how they shine. Ask the children to "echo" what you say, as you read the Bible verse. If outside, blow soap bubbles in the sunshine.)

"Words are windows of the mind,
Or so it seems,

Showing others what's inside:
Our hopes, our fears, our dreams."

Questions to Ponder: **What are the words or pictures inside your mind?**

160

Wonder is the world wet with dew, glistening in the dawn's early sunlight. Wonder is a way of listening to the cosmos, seeing creation as God sees it; seeing the invisible in the presence of God, believing the incredible, becoming what we worship, and celebrating "all we own, we owe." It is a way to invite and entertain and "believe in" the impossible, to see from the heart, and say "Yes" to the Spirit.

Poetry celebrates the beautiful, the unexpected, the temporary, that which causes us to wonder. Poetry is the language for expressing wonder and the values by which we live, our sense of beauty and wonder. "In poetry the child does not understand the values but lives them."[5]

Frederick Buechner, novelist and preacher, wrote, "They (prophet-preachers, poets) put words to both the wonder and the horror of the world, and the words can be looked up in the dictionary or the biblical commentary and can be interpreted, passed on, understood, but because these words are poetry, are image and symbol as well as meaning, are sound and rhythm, maybe above all are passion, they set echoes going the way a choir in a great cathderal [sic] does, only it is we who become the cathedral and in us that the words echo."[6]

Children are the cathedrals of poetry.

The Moon and the Stars

O give thanks to the LORD, . . . who made . . . the moon and stars to rule over the night. (Ps. 136:1-9)

> God fingerpainted clouds
> Upon a piece of sky,
> Then thumbed the moon and stars among them,
> And hung it up to dry.

Questions to Ponder: When you look at the clouds, what do you think or feel? at the moon? the stars? Who created the moon and stars? How does the poem make you feel? What is it trying to say? Who is in charge of the world? How can we "partner" with God?

In the sanctuary invite the children to look at paintings they or other children have created that show the wonder and beauty of creation. Outside of the sanctuary, in an appropriate setting, provide fingerpainting material for the children to create.

Children know there is An Other, Someone responsible for the universe, which is a work of art. Children rest upon the beauty of the world, God's playground, where they are partners with God in caring for the planet. Those who touch children with compassion, they recognize as God "with skin on."

God reveals, and part of our task is to get out of God's way, to be open to the surprises of God. Children experience God's presence and this is the very heart of religion and the miracle of creation is all about us. As we enflesh our experiences of awe and wonder at God's love, children catch our excitement. Our attitudes of adoration for the One who provides the surprises and unexplainable mysteries of life help to create an ambience for awe.

Young children are comfortable with the metaphor of God as "Creator," this "name" for the Mystery whom we cannot see but who is the very source and meaning of life. Biblical people named God by what God did.

Knowledge of God is not information about God but a relationship of love with God. It is not as important to know as it is to provide an atmosphere of love and wonder, gratitude and joy, celebration and thanksgiving for the gift of life and love.

When I Look at the Heavens

When I look at your heavens,
the work of your fingers,
the moon and the stars that
you have established . . . (Ps. 8:3)

When I look at the heavens,
the seas and the sands,
the moon and the flowers
that cover the lands,
the great gray mountain
that silent stands
forever . . .
When I see all the cattle,
the oxen and sheep,

the birds of the air,
the fish of the deep,
and know you have put them into our keep

forever . . .
Then I wonder and wonder,
"Who are we?" and why
You have loved us and placed us so high?
"How great is your name, Lord," I cry
Forever!

Questions to Ponder: Who are we? What do you "wonder"? Why does God love us so very much? How do we praise and thank God?

Close your eyes and see God's world in your imagination. (Pause.) What do you see? One of God's surprises is the miracle of our bodies. Think of some of the things our bodies do! (Eyes see, ears hear, heart pumps blood, noses smell, hands feel, tongues taste, and minds imagine.) Sometimes, however, we forget to be glad to God.

God has a wonderful imagination. Think of creating a world with seas and sands, moon and mountains and trees, lakes and oceans, fish and birds, cows and elephants, and people of different colors and shapes and sizes. God is full of surprises!

A full, alive, whole life includes the emotions as well as the intellect. Imagination involves both, accepts the paradoxes of life, rejoices in the rainbow rather than the "pure, white light of truth," and experiences the inner world, the world of possibility.

Wonder

"Consider the lilies of the field, how they grow; they neither toil nor spin."
(Matt. 6:28)

A group of kindergarten children visited the flower garden of a thoughtful neighbor. The spring sun shone brightly on the red, pink, blue, and yellow petals, and the birds seemed to echo the flowers' beauty in song. As the children rounded a corner of boxwood bushes, they came upon a scene of startling beauty: rows and rows of golden daffodils in full bloom. Suddenly they were quiet. No one spoke. In the hushed silence, one of the children asked the teacher, "Can I stand on my knees, Teacher?"

Silently, the children knelt, surrounded by the beauty of God's creation.

Questions to Ponder: Where do you find wonder and beauty?

Bring a rose to let the children see and smell and feel.

Wonder is seeing with the heart. "It is only with the heart that one can see rightly; what is essential is invisible to the eye," the fox explained to the little prince.[7]

Acts of wonder are symbols of the meaning for which all things stand. We are beings in quest of meaning. Why is there a world? Why is there a me? What is the meaning of what happens, of what I do, and who I am? Why am I here? Am I needed? Children need stories that help them relate what they see and hear with God and wonder and the world.

Children experience wonder, which is the foundation for their worship, through beauty and nature, delight and play, wherever they are.

Notes

Celebrating Advent

1. Elaine M. Ward, *Being with God* (Prescott, Ariz.: Educational Ministries, 1988), p. 15. Used with permission.
2. Elaine M. Ward, *In Advent* (Prescott, Ariz.: Educational Ministries, 1993), p. 61. Used with permission.
3. Madeleine L'Engle, *The Rock That Is Higher* (Wheaton, Ill: Harold Shaw Publishers, 1993), p. 218.

Entering the Bible Story

1. Bruno Bettelheim, *The Uses of Enchantment* (New York: Alfred A. Knopf, 1975, 1976), p. 27.
2. Elaine M. Ward, *Children and Biblical Stories* (Prescott, Ariz.: Educational Ministries, 1993), p. 22. Used with permission.
3. Elaine M. Ward, *New Testament Stories* (Prescott, Ariz.: Educational Ministries, 1984), p. 46. Used with permission.

Children

1. Elaine M. Ward, *Feelings Grow Too!* rev. ed. (Prescott, Ariz.: Educational Ministries, 1994), p. 37. Used with permission.

Embracing the Church

1. Elaine M. Ward, *Children and Worship* (Prescott, Ariz.: Educational Ministries, 1993), p. 27. Used with permission.
2. Ibid., p. 1.
3. Elaine M. Ward, *New Testament Stories* (Prescott, Ariz.: Educational Ministries, 1984), p. 13. Used with permission.

Encountering God

1. Hilda Conkling, *Poems by a Little Girl* (New York: J. B. Lippincott, 1920).
2. Elaine M. Ward, *Colors from Story Tree* (Allen, Tex.: Tabor, 1981). Used by permission.

3. C. S. Lewis, *The Magician's Nephew*, vol. 6, *The Chronicles of Narnia* (New York: Collier, 1970), pp. 104-16.

4. Victor Hugo, "Be Like the Bird" from *A Child's Book of Poems* (New York: Grosset, 1969).

Celebrating Lent

1. Tom Boomershine, *Story Journey* (Nashville: Abingdon, 1989), pp. 176-77.

Engaging in Love

1. Madeleine L'Engle, *A Wrinkle in Time* (New York: Dell, 1983), p. 75.

2. Ibid.

3. Elaine M. Ward, *Children and Prayer* (Prescott, Ariz.: Educational Ministries, 1993), p. 24. Used with permission.

Experiencing Wonder

1. Antoine de Saint Exupery, *The Little Prince* (New York: Harcourt, Brace, Jovanovich, 1943, 1971), pp. 96-97.

2. Annie Dillard, *Pilgrim at Tinker Creek* (New York: Bantam, 1982), p. 92.

3. Edward Robinson, *The Original Vision: A Study of the Religious Experience of Children* (New York: Seabury Press, 1983), pp. 12-13.

4. Ibid., pp. 32-33.

5. James Britton, *Prospect and Retrospect*, ed. Gordon M. Pradl (Montclair, N.J.: Boynton Cook Publishers, 1982), p. 19.

6. Frederick Buechner, *Telling the Truth* (San Francisco: Harper & Row, 1981), p. 21.

7. de Saint Exupery, *The Little Prince*, p. 87.

Scripture Index

Genesis
1:1   34, 155
1:3   99
1:11   155
2:7   138
6:8   39
12:1   33
40:8   62

Exodus
3:14*a*   86

Deuteronomy
6:4-5   93
6:5   129

Joshua
24:15   80

1 Samuel
17:45   31

1 Kings
3:5   45

Psalms
2:1   135
8:1*a*   100
8:3   162
8:3-5   73
23:4   89
24:1   151
26:8   77
29:2*b*   9

33:20   71
34:8*a*   159
39:12*a*   142
40:13*b*   146
46:10   15
50:6   135
71:8   143
96:11-12   141
100:3*a*   75
106:1   140
106:44   81
111:1   144
116:1-2   136
118:24   94
136:1-9   161
139:12*c*   139
139:14*a*   64
139:18*b*   133
141:3   148
144:15*b*   65
147:8*b*   152
147:11   157
148:3   160
150:6   158

Proverbs
10:9   59
22:6   122

Ecclesiastes
3:1   90

Isaiah
55:12   69

167